D0598954

Partnering
with Parents
=== *to Ask the* ===
Right Questions

ASCD MEMBER BOOK

Many ASCD members received this book as a member benefit upon its initial release.

Learn more at: **www.ascd.org/memberbooks**

Partnering *with* Parents

—— *to Ask the* ——
Right Questions

A Powerful Strategy for Strengthening School-Family Partnerships

LUZ
SANTANA

DAN
ROTHSTEIN

AGNES
BAIN

Alexandria, VA

1703 N. Beauregard St. • Alexandria, VA 22311-1714 USA
Phone: 800-933-2723 or 703-578-9600 • Fax: 703-575-5400
Website: www.ascd.org • E-mail: member@ascd.org
Author guidelines: www.ascd.org/write

Deborah S. Delisle, *Executive Director;* Robert D. Clouse, *Managing Director, Digital Content & Publications;* Stefani Roth, *Publisher;* Genny Ostertag, *Director, Content Acquisitions;* Julie Houtz, *Director, Book Editing & Production;* Jamie Greene, *Editor;* Masie Chong, *Graphic Designer;* Mike Kalyan, *Manager, Production Services;* Barton Matheson Willse & Worthington, *Typesetter*

Copyright © 2016 Right Question Institute. All rights reserved. It is illegal to reproduce copies of this work in print or electronic format (including reproductions displayed on a secure intranet or stored in a retrieval system or other electronic storage device from which copies can be made or displayed) without the prior written permission of the publisher. By purchasing only authorized electronic or print editions and not participating in or encouraging piracy of copyrighted materials, you support the rights of authors and publishers. Readers who wish to reproduce or republish excerpts of this work in print or electronic format may do so for a small fee by contacting the Copyright Clearance Center (CCC), 222 Rosewood Dr., Danvers, MA 01923, USA (phone: 978-750-8400; fax: 978-646-8600; web: www.copyright.com). To inquire about site licensing options or any other reuse, contact ASCD Permissions at www.ascd.org/permissions, or permissions@ascd.org, or 703-575-5749. For a list of vendors authorized to license ASCD e-books to institutions, see www.ascd.org/epubs. Send translation inquiries to translations@ascd.org.

Right Question® is a trademark of The Right Question Institute.

ASCD® and ASCD LEARN. TEACH. LEAD.® are registered trademarks of ASCD. All other trademarks contained in this book are the property of, and reserved by, their respective owners, and are used for editorial and informational purposes only. No such use should be construed to imply sponsorship or endorsement of the book by the respective owners.

All web links in this book are correct as of the publication date below but may have become inactive or otherwise modified since that time. If you notice a deactivated or changed link, please e-mail books@ascd.org with the words "Link Update" in the subject line. In your message, please specify the web link, the book title, and the page number on which the link appears.

PAPERBACK ISBN: 978-1-4166-2267-3   ASCD product #117011
PDF E-BOOK ISBN: 978-1-4166- 2268-0; see Books in Print for other formats.
Quantity discounts: 10–49, 10%; 50+, 15%; 1,000+, special discounts (e-mail programteam@ascd.org or call 800-933-2723, ext. 5773, or 703-575-5773). For desk copies, go to www.ascd.org/deskcopy.

ASCD Member Book No. FY17-1 (Sep. 2016 PSI+). ASCD Member Books mail to Premium (P), Select (S), and Institutional Plus (I+) members on this schedule: Jan, PSI+; Feb, P; Apr, PSI+; May, P; Jul, PSI+; Aug, P; Sep, PSI+; Nov, PSI+; Dec, P. For current details on membership, see www.ascd.org/membership.

Library of Congress Cataloging-in-Publication Data
Names: Santana, Luz, author. | Rothstein, Dan, author. | Bain, Agnes, author.
Title: Partnering with parents to ask the right questions : a powerful strategy for strengthening school-family partnerships / Luz Santana, Dan Rothstein, and Agnes Bain.
Description: Alexandria, VA : ASCD, 2016. | Includes bibliographical references and index.
    Identifiers: LCCN 2016023837 (print) | LCCN 2016035307 (ebook) | ISBN 9781416622673 (pbk.) |
    ISBN 97814166 22680 (PDF e-book) | ISBN 9781416622680 (PDF)
Subjects: LCSH: Home and school.
Classification: LCC LC225 .R65 2016 (print) | LCC LC225 (ebook) | DDC 371.19/2—dc23
LC record available at https://lccn.loc.gov/2016023837

25 24 23 22 21 20 19 18 17 16   1 2 3 4 5 6 7 8 9 10 11 12

To the parents in Lawrence, MA, who got us started
and to the educators and parents who will build
strong partnerships in many more communities.

Partnering *with* Parents *to Ask the* Right Questions

Acknowledgments

We are grateful to the parents in Lawrence, MA, who more than two decades ago provided the first insight that shaped the work that led to this book. Many people helped get this work started in Lawrence, including parent leaders Nancy Rodriguez, Barbara Hendricks, Jose Rodriguez, and Wendy Gardner; municipal colleagues Ana Rodriguez, Carmen Schumann, Grecia Alemany, Patricia A. Driscoll, Richard Kobayashi, David Bain, and Patricia Karl; and consultants to the Annie E. Casey Foundation Erik Butler, Manuel Gutierrez, Pauline Lipman, Joe Onosko, and Gary Wehlage.

We continued our learning as we began to partner with community organizations, human service agencies, and parent involvement programs, including the Latino Parents Association in Boston, MA; the Paterson (NJ) Education Fund; the Prichard Committee for Academic Excellence (KY); the Center for Collaborative Planning (Sacramento, CA); the Family Resource Coalition (Chicago, IL); Teaching for Change (Washington, DC); as well as many federally funded Parent Information and Resource Centers around the country. We greatly benefited from doing direct work with Margaret Gallagher and the parent liaisons from the Cambridge, MA, public schools.

Ana Rodriguez, Krystal Robinson, Ana Karchmer, Patricia A. Nelson, and Naomi Campbell made valuable contributions to the development of our strategy across multiple fields. We benefited greatly from the wisdom of Amy Shine Jones, Donna Muncey, Cheryl Almeida, and Christine Pizer, whose assessment and evaluation work helped identify key lessons from both parents and educators. We were also fortunate at the beginning of our journey to learn from Jane Vella, a truly great adult educator who taught us so very much about "teaching to learn" and "learning to teach," as well as about the power of saying "thank you."

We were fortunate to receive strong support at various times from foundations that funded our work with parents in communities around the country, including the Boston Foundation, the Wallace Funds (then known as the DeWitt Wallace Reader's Digest Fund), the Joyce Foundation, the Rhode Island Foundation, the Rockefeller Brothers Fund, the Barr Foundation, Jane's Trust, and, at a particularly challenging moment, the Germanacos Foundation.

We are grateful to our current funders who have provided critical support to continue our work with parents as part of the Right Question Institute's overall commitment to Microdemocracy. Mary and Ted Wendell of the Hummingbird Fund have provided generous, consistent support that made possible our work in multiple fields and over this past year allowed us to focus on writing this book. John Esterle has been a strong advocate for us helping secure stable, multi-year support from The Whitman Institute. As we move ahead, we also look forward to combining school-family partnerships with our parallel work strengthening the capacity of teachers to teach students to ask their own questions as part of the Million Classrooms Campaign, supported by the Sir John Templeton Foundation.

We have also benefited greatly from major donor support from Diane Englander and Mark Underberg, Franklin M. and Ellen P.

Fisher, Stephen Quatrano and Dr. Doreen Karoll, and Nathan Rothstein of Project Repat.

The board of directors of the Right Question Institute is made up of a remarkable group of idealistic, visionary, and determined people who have been full partners in this work for many years, have helped steer the ship, provided moral support, and kept the lights on! We are grateful to each of them: President of the Board Mary Wendell, Vice President Diane Englander, Clerk Macky Buck, and members Gail Fuller, David Guberman, Shonak Patel, Stephen Quatrano, Dr. Carol Robey, and Enid Shapiro. We also appreciate the encouragement to pursue our school-family partnership work from past board members Richard Weissbourd of the Harvard Graduate School of Education; Ron Walker, CEO of the Coalition of Schools Educating Boys of Color; and Franklin M. Fisher, professor emeritus, MIT.

Specific chapters were greatly enhanced by insights from Elizabeth Bain, a school psychologist in Lawrence, MA; and Ariela Rothstein, a high school history teacher in Brooklyn, NY. We have benefited from conversations over the years with Julia Coffman and M. Elena Lopez of the Harvard Family Research Project; our collaboration with Commissioner Virginia Barry; and colleagues Mary Earick and Art Ellison at the New Hampshire Department of Education, Irv Richardson of NEA-NH, and leaders in the field of parent involvement, including Karen Mapp, Ann Henderson, Don Davies, Vivian Johnson, Tony Wagner, Mary Harrison, Steve LeClair, Lynne Simons, Kate Miller, Theresa Jensen, Kate Gill Kressley, Bryan Samuels, Bev Raimondo, Carol Edelin, Ethel Seiderman, the late Bob Sexton, and the late Barbara Shaw. Natasha Freidus of Creative Narrations provided superb documentation of what parents in many communities were learning, thinking, and feeling as they acquired the skills to participate more effectively in their children's education. We also appreciate the encouragement and support from faculty at the

Harvard Graduate School of Education, including Richard Murnane who first wrote about our work with parents in his 1995 book *Teaching the New Basic Skills*, Karen Mapp and graduate students in her courses on family and community engagement, and Meira Levinson who convened a colloquium at Harvard on the theory and practice of the Right Question Institute.

While working on this book, we had strong support from staff and interns at the Right Question Institute. We are indebted to Andrew Minigan, Education and Research Project Coordinator, who goes above and beyond the call of duty and brings great energy and wisdom to work every day. Lavada Berger and John Sessler provided additional key support over the past year. We are also grateful for the smart digital strategy and web management work done by Morgan Schwartz, which allows more people to access the Right Question Strategy. We greatly appreciate all of the hard work from our interns, led by Mikah Farbo's diligent research and bibliographic skills with additional insights and support from Codie Kane, Kelly Wallace, Diana Morrill, Aisha Suara, Sara Peck, Neil Alacha, Danielle McPeak, Solange Azor, Kendall Gedeon, Gavin Hui, and Betsy Waisel.

We are pleased to partner with ASCD to bring the Right Question Strategy to its extensive network of educators around the country. Genny Ostertag took the initiative to get things started. Susan Hills, acquisitions editor, always communicated thoughtfully and respectfully and then helped deliver the manuscript into the experienced and skillful editorial hands of Jamie Greene. To all of the above and our dear families and friends, we say thank you.

Luz   Dan   Agnes

Introduction:
Making Meaningful School-Family
Partnerships Easier

The educators and parents you will meet in this book quietly do something quite remarkable. They demonstrate how to work together for the benefit of all students by using a simple and cost-effective partnership strategy.

The examples we present are drawn largely from low- and moderate-income communities around the country where both educators and parents are asked to do too much with too few resources. Each day, they must confront the painful reality, as the economists Greg Duncan and Richard Murnane (2014) have documented, where economic inequality is increasing, with harmful effects on the housing stability, physical and emotional health, safety, and general well-being of children—all of which makes the work of educators that much more difficult.

In this context, schools are too often unfairly expected to single-handedly solve the problem of disparities in achievement across racial and socioeconomic lines at a time when inequality beyond the school walls is sharply increasing (Lareau, 2003). The people who send the children to school—parents, foster parents, guardians, and grandparents—are also in a difficult position. Struggling to put food on the table and ensure the safety of their children while working one or two jobs or seeking employment in order to pay the bills, they can too readily be blamed for not being involved enough in their children's education. The call for greater parent involvement or family engagement has to walk a fine line to ensure that the problems students might have in school are not pinned on their parents' lack of participation (Edmonds, 1979).

The challenge of improving education for all students requires us to directly address the "opportunity gap" and an inequitable distribution of resources rather than focus solely on the consequences it produces, which have come to be labeled as the achievement gap. The opportunity gap—the need to ensure sufficient resources for schools as well as families—is a responsibility our entire society must shoulder. It should not be added to the burdens already placed on educators and parents (Schott Foundation for Public Education, n.d.).

So, instead of adding more demands, this book presents a modest resource to lessen the burden on educators and families who are pressured to somehow solve overwhelming problems on their own. Over the past 20 years, working in communities across the country, we have carefully developed, tested, and refined a strategy that makes it *easier* for more educators and families to work together to help struggling individual students and to become strong allies in advocating for greater equity and increased opportunities for all students. The Right Question School-Family Partnership Strategy (the Right Question Strategy) cannot solve, on its own, the complex problems related to the achievement gap. It can, however, be an efficient and effective means to mobilize more hands on deck so the key adults in a student's life work together constructively. This partnership does not guarantee success, but we know that the absence of a strong partnership can exacerbate the problem (Lawrence-Lightfoot, 2003).

It might sound absurd to talk about making it *easier* to create a strong school-family partnership. Who has time and resources for this very complex task? We regularly hear classroom teachers, counselors, assistant principals, principals, and district leaders voice, in one way or another, a common lament:

We wish we had more parents who were actively involved in their children's education. We have to spend about 95 percent of any "parent-focused time" with a very small number of parents whose children are having serious learning or discipline problems. We wish we saw more of all the other parents, but we've tried to reach out and haven't gotten much of a response. And there are always so many other demands on us that take all of our time. Our job, every day, is to ensure that all of our students learn. Given the many challenges students face, we also try to provide social and emotional support that not only helps them feel better and more comfortable in school but also enhances their chances of academic success. We try to provide support to one another because this is a hard job, and we often feel like we're on the edge of failing. We are constantly being judged and evaluated based on how well our students do on state-mandated tests. Their test scores become "our" scores, and we are compared to schools and districts in higher-income communities where students face fewer challenges in their lives and there is strong parent involvement in their education.

In those same communities, we often hear these comments from parents:

> *I wish I could make sure my kids do well in school. I know how important it is, but I don't really know what I can do. When I go to meetings, I'm always worried that they'll tell me my kids aren't behaving or that they're not getting good grades. I'm not sure what I can do. I'm doing my best working two jobs, or sometimes I'm out of work looking for a job, or I'm just plain out of luck. When my kids bring home homework, I can't really help them. If I do go to meetings at the school (and it can be hard just to get to the school), I just sit there and listen. I don't even know what to ask. So I kind of stay away from it all and just hope my kids behave and the school teaches my kids what they need.*

A few districts, here and there, have found a way to secure significant additional resources, create new infrastructures, and hire additional personnel to offer programs for parents—including "parent universities," or parent leadership programs (Mapp, 2011; Molnar, 2013). The vast majority of overburdened schools, however, have little time and very few resources to commit to engaging more parents in the life of the schools and the education of their children.

One Strategy, Two Skills, Three Roles

This book is for educators in schools and districts with too few resources and who, nevertheless, want to tap into the great value of creating a strong partnership with their students' families. To make it easier to use our strategy for that goal, we always keep this question in mind: *What is the maximum that can be achieved by teaching the minimum?*

We are not providing an exhaustive or comprehensive educational program for parents that will provide information and support for addressing every possible issue that might come up along a student's K–12 journey. Instead, we sharply focus on just a few key factors that are universally relevant and have a transformative power when put into action. Specifically, we have seen that strong partnerships emerge when parents learn to play three key roles effectively:

- They support their children's education at home.
- They monitor their progress.
- They advocate for them when necessary.

How best, then, to develop parents' ability to play these roles? Again, with the goal of keeping it as simple as possible, we have learned that when parents learn just the following two skills, they greatly improve their ability to support, monitor, and advocate:

- They formulate and use questions effectively.
- They participate effectively in decisions that affect them.

We will introduce you to simple, easy-to-learn and easy-to-implement methods for teaching these two skills that in turn lead to parents playing the three key roles that enable stronger partnerships. We emphasize that we are offering a *strategy* that can be integrated into your regular workflow rather than a *program* that requires new infrastructure, additional personnel, and more funding. The only "cost" to you is to make a commitment to invest in building the capacity of all parents to ask better questions and participate in decisions that affect them and their children. As you begin to implement the Right Question Strategy, you will soon see how you can continuously adapt and improve it for different purposes so you and your family partners will reap both short- and long-term payoffs for the investment you make up front.

The Unusual Source of a Profound Insight

We believe that the great value and transformative impact of deliberately teaching "just" two skills is due to the unusual source of the original insight that guides the entire Right Question Strategy. The insight first appeared on the scene a little more than two decades ago. We were working on a drop-out prevention program funded by the Annie E. Casey Foundation in Lawrence, Massachusetts—a former thriving textile industry hub that suffered a severe economic downturn when the factories left town in search of cheaper labor. Our task was to find ways to get parents more involved in their children's education. In conversation after conversation with parents in the community, primarily low- and moderate-income Latino and white parents, we repeatedly heard that they didn't participate in their children's education and didn't go to the schools because they "didn't even know what to ask."

We interpreted the problem as not having questions to ask. We thought we could solve that by giving a list of questions to the parents. We began to observe that one week, parents would come to us and say they didn't know what their children were supposed to be doing for homework. We gave them a list of questions to ask about homework. The next week, they came and said they didn't know what to ask about a new school disciplinary policy. We drafted another list of questions for them to ask about disciplinary policies. Then, a week later, a few parents came and wanted questions to ask because their children had been referred for testing for an Individualized Education Program.

The pattern quickly became all too clear. We were making parents *more* dependent on us. We thought we had an answer to the problem—give them questions—but we were wrong.

The problem was not about the lack of questions. They were actually sharing a profound insight by naming "not knowing what to ask" as a fundamental yet overlooked obstacle to effective participation in any setting. However, like many an original insight, it can seem so obvious that its importance will be completely overlooked. The parents helped us understand that the ability to ask questions is not only a sophisticated thinking skill but also an essential advocacy one. They helped us realize that we needed to stop giving out lists of questions and figure out how to teach this seemingly simple but profoundly important skill. That was no small task.

There was no easily accessible model. Even though Socrates had demonstrated the power of questions more than a couple of millennia ago, the actual practice for teaching other people to ask their own questions—and not leave the skill only in the hands of the wisest person in the room—had not advanced much (Rothstein, 2012).

The assumption that the skill of question formulation is really the province of only the highly educated was made even clearer when Kate Zernike (2002) of *The New York Times* interviewed college presidents, asking them what a student should know after four years of higher education. The presidents of Bard College and the University of Illinois said because there is "so much knowledge and information" that cannot possibly be entirely learned and absorbed, the best thing colleges can do is ensure that students can "ask strategic questions" and find a way to get to the "right questions."

Those were college presidents talking about students in college. Long before they were interviewed, we were asking ourselves if such a sophisticated thinking and learning skill could be taught on the fly as part of school efforts to engage parents. We got to work trying to figure out how to quickly teach this important skill in a way that *all* people, those with little education and those with lots of it, could improve their ability to ask their own questions.

It took a good many years, lots of trial, and many errors, but we eventually figured out how to teach a sophisticated thinking skill in a simple way. We developed the Question Formulation Technique

(QFT), a process that allows anyone who uses it to learn how to *produce* their own questions, *improve* their questions, and *strategize* about how to use them.

As we continued our work and research on the ground, we learned that the parents who were most effective in using their new skills began to ask better questions about decisions affecting them and their children. Based on our lessons from their actions, we teased out another accessible, easily teachable tool: the Framework for Accountable Decision Making (FADM).

The FADM also does something deceptively simple: it starts by defining a decision as the "selection of one option among two or more options." This explanation emphasizes that a decision involves selecting an option. This then facilitates the use of three basic criteria when looking at any decision—specifically

- The reasons for a decision.
- The process for making the decision.
- The role of the person(s) affected by the decision in the decision-making process.

In Chapter 2, you will see the full description of the Support, Monitor, and Advocate (SMA) Model, the QFT, and the FADM. Then, in the case studies that follow, you will see how educators and parents use different aspects of the Right Question Strategy to help build their partnerships. In the Appendix, there are additional materials that will make it easy to teach the content of the strategy, prepare to use the strategy, and facilitate the strategy when working with parents.

An Evidence-Based Strategy: Data from Many Fields and Communities

The QFT and the FADM have been used across a range of fields and in a diverse set of communities. The results are consistently similar:

people who had previously not participated effectively in key decisions were now actively using their new skills, participating, speaking up, and partnering constructively with professionals. For example, in a randomized control study funded by the National Institutes of Health, the Right Question Strategy was taught to patients at community mental health centers in low-income Latino communities. The results were impressive—patients became up to three times as "activated" and engaged as they had been previously. This success led to a national expansion of the strategy (Alegría et al., 2008). This was followed by research and implementation projects including areas as diverse as New York City community health centers, where the Right Question Strategy was shown to be highly effective after being taught to patients in just 7–10 minutes while they were in the waiting rooms (Deen, Lu, Rothstein, Santana, & Gold, 2011; Lu, Deen, Rothstein, Santana, & Gold, 2011). The use of the strategy to activate patients continues to grow in places ranging from the Massachusetts Office of Refugees and Immigrants (in collaboration with the Massachusetts Department of Public Health, Division of Global Populations and Infectious Disease Prevention to promote engagement and retention in care for refugees) to the Kaiser Permanente Health Care System on the island of Oahu in Hawaii (Olinger & Nelson, 2015).

The QFT has proven to be an effective resource for educators in K–12 classrooms and in higher education. Since the publication of *Make Just One Change: Teach Students to Ask Their Own Questions* (Rothstein & Santana, 2011), there has been an explosion of use of the QFT in classrooms around the world. In more than 100,000 classrooms, teachers are finding that students who learn to ask their own questions by using the QFT are more engaged, take greater ownership of their learning, and are learning more deeply than ever before. Educators have also adapted the QFT for their specific teaching and learning goals in the classroom (Rothstein, Santana, &

Minigan, 2015). Teachers, principals, districts, and state leaders have led the way in this widespread adoption of the QFT—from a 3rd grade teacher in a Los Angeles elementary school starting a book club, to a teacher's union leader and a state commissioner of education in New Hampshire introducing and supporting use of the QFT in all Title I schools across the state, to school districts across Appalachian eastern Kentucky.

In 2015, as the school was in the process of revamping its program of studies for first- and second-year medical students, Harvard Medical School reached out to us to learn more about how to teach the skill of question formulation to all people, including students like theirs who have excelled at answering other people's questions. The robustness of the technique has been demonstrated for a variety of purposes across grades and subject areas, with students in urban, suburban, and rural areas and in border communities with large immigrant populations.

Using the Right Question Strategy to Build Partnerships with Parents

In 1995, we were selected in the very first cohort of grantees to receive funds to establish Parent Information and Resource Centers as part of the Goals 2000 U.S. Department of Education. Working with sites primarily in rural communities and small cities around Massachusetts, we saw a sharp increase in schools and families working collaboratively. Schools and community agencies made a commitment to invest in the capacity of parents to better support, monitor, and advocate for their children's education.

The impact across many communities was quite moving. In a workshop at a homeless shelter in Cambridge, MA, one mother shared how "learning to ask questions gives me the confidence to meet with teachers. I was always afraid of going and looking stupid and that would be bad for my kids. Now I feel like I know that it's OK to ask questions and I know what I want to ask." This kind of impact was widespread across the state as evaluations showed that there was a dramatic increase in parent communications with teachers (Black, 1998).

Our work began to be recognized nationally, and we were also in the first cohort of "parent involvement" grantees funded by the Wallace Funds (then the DeWitt Wallace–Reader's Digest Fund). We began to work with other Parent Information and Resource Centers around the country in Rhode Island, Indiana, and New Mexico. In Kentucky, the Prichard Committee for Academic Excellence, a non-profit education and advocacy organization, collaborated with the Jefferson County Public Schools to invite us to train parent liaisons in the schools to work more effectively with parents (Sexton, 2004). Our work with them was the forerunner to their highly respected Commonwealth Institute for Parent Leadership, which has been a strong voice on behalf of strengthening schools and increasing funding and resources across the state for many years.

In a study they commissioned with support from Hayes Mizell of the Edna McConnell Clark Foundation, University of Louisville researchers found that there was significantly increased communication with teachers and administrators and nearly a doubling of the number of parents who felt a strong sense of accomplishment in their interactions with school staff *after* learning to ask their own questions (Ruscoe & Gaus, 1997). The parent liaisons who worked in the schools were also determined to teach the Right Question Strategy to parents wherever they could find them—in public housing developments, church groups, homeless shelters, and parent conference days at the schools. In the Wayside Shelter for Families, one mother reflected on what she had learned and said, "Now, I will do whatever it takes to get the information to help my child."

Theresa Jensen, one of the most respected principals in the Louisville, KY, school district, worked with parent liaisons and parent volunteers to offer workshops to all incoming parents at Englehard Elementary School. "We need," she asserted, "more parents asking questions. It helps us and helps their children" (Garrett, 1997). She was but one of many school leaders around the country who began to support and promote use of the Right Question Strategy to build stronger partnerships with families. One elementary school teacher in central Massachusetts, for example, observed, "We have never had as productive a conversation with parents as we have had with parents who learned to ask their own questions."

Schools also began to get more support in this effort to engage parents from social service agencies and community organizations. In Sacramento, CA, Faye Kennedy of the Center for Collaborative Planning (who works with immigrant parents of English language learners), said the process helps hesitant and shy parents "find their voice. They know they don't need me to speak up for them. They can do it themselves." One Mexican immigrant mother with whom she worked described how learning to ask her own questions made her better prepared. "You know what you want to know, and when you know *that* you can look for a way to get it." Parents are able to get what they want because they have the skills that the Right Question Strategy builds to help them participate in decisions affecting their children (Nelson, 2003).

In the 20 years since we began teaching the Right Question Strategy for building school-family partnerships, we have also seen that the language of our strategy has influenced the national discourse about best practices when working with parents. The Harvard Family Research Project reported that the Right Question Strategy "provides a simple methodology of framing questions that parents can use in teacher conferences and parent meetings. Parents can be supported in developing leadership skills to monitor school reform" (Weiss, Kreider, Lopez, & Chatman-Nelson, 2005, p. xxii).

In her courses on working with families at the Harvard Graduate School of Education, Karen Mapp, a nationally recognized expert on family engagement, often devotes time to introducing her students to the Right Question Strategy, which she also has highlighted as a "best practice" that recognizes the strengths of families and what they can offer schools. Anne Henderson, who is also a national leader in the field of family engagement, cites the Right Question Strategy as a best practice in family engagement in her book *Beyond the Bake Sale: The Essential Guide to Family-School Partnerships* (Henderson, Mapp, Johnson, & Davies, 2007). In their Framework for Family-School Partnerships, the U.S. Department of Education eventually adopted new guidelines for working with families that included our original language emphasizing three roles parents can play in their children's education (Mapp & Kuttner, 2013).

Over the course of the past two decades there has been a change in how schools define families'—and more specifically, parents'—roles in education (Epstein, 2001; Haskins & Adams, 1983; Henderson & Mapp, 2002). The shift from a separation between involvement at home and participation at school to a more active and collaborative role stems from the schools' understanding that every parent has something to benefit the school. It is important to note that even though the terms *parent involvement* and *family engagement* are commonly used, they are meant to represent the wide range of adults who might be responsible for a child's education, which can include guardians, foster parents, grandparents, and even older siblings. We are emphasizing here, much as Joyce Epstein of Johns Hopkins has advocated, the use of the term *partnership*, which raises the level of interaction from "involvement" or "engagement" to a collaborative relationship. We feel that captures more accurately what happens when the Right Question Strategy is deployed. In short, we agree with this definition of the working relationship: "[A] shared responsibility for the education of a child, between parents, schools, and communities, and is rooted in an asset-based understanding of the strengths of each part of the partnership" (Kammen et al., 2014, p. 9).

The Structure of This Book

In a series of case studies, we illustrate how the Right Question Strategy can help remove many of the traditional obstacles to more effective parent participation. In Appendix B, we provide additional teaching and learning materials that are designed to enable readers to learn the strategy one day and implement it the next. This apparent simplicity, however, belies the rigor and discipline in the strategy.

In Chapter 1, we fully unpack the Right Question Strategy and illustrate how its components fit together. Then, in each case chapter, inspired by all the people with whom we have worked, we present an issue that brings into sharp focus how the absence of effective parent engagement exacerbates the problem of inequity. We created composite case studies in order to capture as many of the parents' and educators' contributions as possible and lay out how the strategy can be quickly implemented and flexibly applied. A teacher will help a parent address the issue of a child not doing his homework. A school will engage parents around the issue of bullying. A parent liaison will help a parent prepare to fully participate in her legal role at an IEP meeting. A school district will bring parents into a conversation about equity and how to improve educational outcomes for all students. And a community of primarily immigrant parents of English language learners (ELLs) using skills taught by a staff member from a social service agency will mobilize around a crisis in their children's school to ferret out and hold accountable the complex layers of public decision-making bodies that affect the opportunities and resources made available to its children. Each case study includes a description of a significant challenge and a brief discussion of traditional approaches and their limitations. We then present how the Right Question Strategy can be helpful. The composite case studies are drawn from the hundreds of places where the strategy has been implemented around the country.

As we pieced the stories together from hundreds of examples, we were inspired anew with the intelligence, determination, and pluck of both educators and parents who, each day, face great challenges in their work and their lives. Their stories are so impressive that they could trigger a perception that they are just "too good to be true." It is, indeed, accurate to describe them as best practices. They are not, however, impossible-to-achieve practices. Nor are they the kind of such extraordinary best practices that can leave one feeling incapable of emulating them. On the contrary, the case studies show how, in each situation, the use of the strategy is a lesson from and a replication of its use in some other setting by someone else. This is precisely how the strategy has been shared around the country: from trusted source to trusted source.

We also adopt an unusual practice in introducing the key characters in the case studies. We use initials in place of names. You'll meet people like Ms. R, Ms. S, Mr. M, and people who are identified as a father, mother, neighbor, and friend. Why didn't we just use the standard practice of pseudonyms? Here's the reason. When relaying some of the stories appearing in the case studies, we occasionally hear negative responses from people working in demographically similar communities. They say, "Oh, *our* parents could never do this," as if the ability to learn to ask questions and participate in decisions is simply beyond their intelligence level. Over the past two decades, in community after community, we have witnessed the extraordinary intelligence and capability of people from whom not much is expected as they begin to think for themselves, advocate effectively for their families and communities, and participate effectively in their children's education. We are presenting a range of examples that are universally relevant and demonstrate just how much people who have not previously participated can do to help their children and partner with educators. We need to keep the focus on their actions, not on their names and whatever associations that might provoke. We use initials, therefore, to emphasize that the ability to learn the sophisticated thinking skills presented in the case studies is not beyond the reach of anyone, no matter what anyone may think their names or the spelling of their names might represent.

We encourage you, as you read about the people in the case studies, to think about the great untapped potential that exists among so many of the families of the students you serve. You can create partnerships to address the issues discussed in the case studies and much, much more. The use of the Right Question Strategy is not limited to the few topics, grade levels, and challenges described in this book.

There are key moments in each of the stories presented in this book when both educators and parents discover just how quickly they can transform their limited interactions into an active collaboration. Parents who were previously disengaged enjoy their newfound ability to support their children's education, monitor their progress, and even advocate for their children when necessary. Educators also benefit by having a strong partner outside the classroom. As parents learn to better support, monitor, and advocate for their children's education, they will not only work more effectively with individual teachers but also become advocates for helping schools obtain the resources they need to best serve their students. They become both powerful individual collaborators and a collective partner for change.

Creating New Sources of Expertise

We have, over the course of two decades of wide-ranging work, become experts of a sort. Our expertise is really about our ability to learn from others and then translate those lessons into teaching and learning methods that promote great independent thought and personal and political efficacy. Of course, we have arrived at this level of expertise because we have met the criteria about what constitutes an expert as set by the Nobel Prize–winning physicist Niels Bohr. An expert, according to Bohr, is "a person who has found out by his own painful experience all the mistakes that one can make" and there are no more to make (quoted in Teller, 1954, p. 62).

We've made many, many mistakes on the way to creating a deceptively simple strategy that is easy to implement and can build strong school-family partnerships. We not only have learned from parents and educators, as described here, but also have learned a great deal from one another and have benefited from the diversity of experiences and backgrounds that we bring to our team.

We invite you to benefit from the lessons we have learned (through much trial and many errors) through years of trying to make this strategy as simple as possible. We encourage you to take the wisdom and expertise of the educators and parents from whom you will hear in this book and then share it with colleagues and parents in your communities. By helping parents enhance their ability to ask questions, participate in decisions, and learn to support their children's education, monitor their progress, and advocate for them, you help build their ability to actively and fully work on the wide range of challenges that appear throughout a child's educational journey. Make that investment and you will experience, as the educators and parents in this book demonstrate, great new joy in your school community. It is an investment that has an immediate pay-off and significant long-term value. You will be, of course, directly helping your students, but you are doing even more than that, without adding to your burdens. You will be building a stronger community. Furthermore, as educators working in one of the most important institutions in a democratic society—the public school—you will be strengthening democracy by making it possible for more people to confidently ask questions and participate in decisions that affect them.

We mentioned earlier that we offer this book as a modest contribution to help lessen the burdens on both educators and parents and make it easier to build strong school-family partnerships. We expect, however, that the outcomes will be anything but modest. Just as the lessons in this book were acquired from the people with whom we have worked in the past, we expect to learn a lot in the future from you. You will become the new experts (making, we're sure, fewer mistakes than we made), and your work will inspire others and make a difference on behalf of all the students you serve.

1

The Right Question School-Family Partnership Strategy

The Right Question School-Family Partnership Strategy (Right Question Strategy) is a deceptively simple strategy that can be used with all parents, including those who are already active and those who have not participated previously, to greatly enhance their ability to partner more effectively with educators on students' behalf. It has just three core components: one set of specific roles for parents to play and two skills that allow them to play those roles effectively. Research in different fields and diverse communities has shown that the Right Question Strategy, despite its simplicity, quickly and efficiently produces profound cognitive, affective, and behavioral changes, as you will see in the following chapters.

The strategy is designed to allow for a modular approach to make it easier to implement. There are many ways to mix and match the three components in your work with parents and families. The case study chapters (Chapter 2–6) demonstrate the strategy's flexibility by exploring a variety of adaptations depending on different challenges, goals, ages and other demographics, and student needs.

The three key components are as follows.

1. Question Formulation Technique (QFT): Developing the Skill of Question Formulation

- A step-by-step process that allows parents to produce their own questions, improve their questions, and strategize on how to use their questions.
- The QFT also makes it possible to use three distinct thinking abilities in one process:
  - » Divergent thinking
  - » Convergent thinking
  - » Metacognitive thinking

2. Framework for Accountable Decision Making (FADM): Developing the Skill of Participating Effectively in Decisions

- A clear analytical structure that allows parents to focus sharply on key decisions, ask their own questions, and apply specific criteria for ensuring accountable decision making.
- Use of the FADM begins with defining a *decision* as the selection of one option among two or more options and then using that definition to identify key decisions.
- Three criteria to apply to decisions:
  - » There is a legitimate *reason* for the decision.
  - » There is a transparent *process* for the decision.
  - » Anyone affected by the decision has an opportunity to participate—to play a *role* in the decision-making process.

3. **The Support, Monitor, and Advocate Model: Partnering Effectively with Educators**

Parents can play the following three roles:
- *Support* their children's education.
- *Monitor* their progress.
- *Advocate* for them when necessary.

These components of the Right Question Strategy constitute the core content, the *what* of the strategy, but to use the strategy most effectively requires a clear understanding of the *how*—that is, the principles and best practices related to how the strategy is taught, facilitated, and shared (Karchmer, 2010). The entire Right Question Strategy is grounded in a strengths-based approach that recognizes the potential of all parents, regardless of their literacy level or background, to ask good questions, participate effectively in decisions, and partner constructively with schools. Teaching resources and templates to support your use of the strategy in a range of settings can be found in Appendix B.

The Question Formulation Technique (QFT)

The QFT provides a rigorous process that helps all people develop their ability to ask their own questions. The technique has been effectively used in a variety of fields and communities and with adults across a range of educational levels. A full description of how it is used by teachers with students in the classroom can be found in our book *Make Just One Change: Teach Students to Ask Their Own Questions* (Rothstein & Santana, 2011). On the website of the Right Question Institute, you can also access many more examples of how teachers across the world implement the QFT with great success.

The full QFT process includes five general steps. In those five steps, parents (1) produce their own questions, (2) work with and improve their own questions, (3) prioritize their questions, (4) strategize on next steps and how to use the questions, and (5) reflect on what they have learned by working with their questions.

It is not necessary to always use all five steps together, for there are situations where one or several of the steps are more important to use than others. In the case studies included in this book, you will see this flexibility and how educators use the QFT differently depending on the setting, their goals, and the people with whom they are working.

Preparing to Use the QFT and Facilitate the Process with Parents

The QFT is a simple process, but using it well requires some preparation and implementation is enhanced by specific best practices that ensure its maximum benefit when working with colleagues and parents. We will provide specific examples of how to do this, but before we do that, here are the basic steps in your use of the QFT.

In Step 1, you present four rules for producing questions, and parents then discuss the challenges they might face in following them. Then they start asking questions about a Question Focus you have created. In Step 2, parents categorize their questions as open- or closed-ended, discuss the advantages and disadvantages of both kinds of questions, and practice changing questions from one type to the other. In Step 3, you provide prioritization instructions that will guide how parents work with their questions and prioritize them. In Step 4, parents strategize about how they plan to use their questions as they discuss their "next steps." In Step 5, parents reflect on what they have learned by working with their own questions and how they can use what they learned.

Step 1: Produce Your Own Questions

Determine a Question Focus

A Question Focus is a catalyst for parents' questions. Designing the Question Focus (QFocus) begins with the purpose and end goal in mind; do you want to use a Question Focus to start the question-asking process about a specific issue, to set an agenda, to problem solve, or for another purpose? You can design a QFocus with any kind of goal in mind, but you should try to keep it as simple as possible, and you should assess it—test it out—to see if it is compelling enough to stimulate multiple lines of questioning.

The QFocus can be drawn from actual situations parents are facing—a child not making expected progress, a child being referred for a special education evaluation, a child at risk of being held back, or broader topics such as academic standards, safety, the school environment, or changes at the school. The QFocus should be designed with enough "hooks" to grab parents' attention or create a sense of urgency, such as "Your child is being referred for an evaluation" or "There will be changes made on how a student's progress will be measured at your child's school."

It is important when designing a Question Focus to consider how to take a topic that might be too broad and sharpen it; for example, going from "new school policies" to "New school policies on grading will be created this year." The latter is more likely to stimulate a flow of questions.

You will see just how this plays out in Chapter 2 when a teacher considers how best to use the QFT with a student's mother in order to engage her as a partner in solving a problem. In that scenario, the child has suddenly stopped doing his homework even though he had always turned it in on time. The teacher reaches out to the boy's mother to set up a meeting and plans to use the QFT to engage her as a partner in problem solving. The teacher got to work thinking about some Question Focus examples. She knew that she had to come up with multiple options rather than just the first one that came to mind.

After she came up with several, she reviewed them. The first one, "S is not doing his homework," might immediately put the mother on the defensive, as if it were the mother's fault that her son was not doing his homework. She looked at another: "Something seems to have changed about S." This one might also strike fear in the heart of the mother, sounding all too worrisome. Then she thought about another factual statement: "Three times in the past two weeks S did not turn in his homework." This one might work, without giving the impression that S *never* does his homework. She compared it to another one, "S seems to be having trouble doing his homework."

The QFocus highlighting how many times in the last two weeks the homework wasn't done could definitely start some questioning. She decided, however, to go with the simpler one, which was more observational in tone. The word *seems* left some wiggle room for interpretation and discussion and was less harsh than declaring a problem. Its tone also seemed to invite the mother into the thinking process in order to help the teacher figure out how best to help the student.

There is an art to designing the Question Focus. Teachers report that although it is a different way of working—it's a small shift in practice from asking questions of students or parents—it grows on them as they see how it stimulates new thinking and more engagement. It also gets easier to design an effective Question Focus the more you practice.

An exploration of the QFocus and a step-by-step process on how to design it can be found in Appendix B.

Discuss the Rules for Producing Questions

There are four rules for producing questions. When you present them to parents, request that they think about and discuss what might be difficult about following them.

1. Ask as many questions as you can.
2. Do not stop to discuss, judge, or answer the questions.
3. Write down every question exactly as stated.
4. Change any statements into questions.

As shown in Figure 1.1, these rules go much further than simply asking, "Do you have any questions?" or saying, "Ask some questions." Instead, the rules provide a clear structure that shows *how* parents can generate their own questions. It took us close to eight years to come

Figure 1.1
Contexts for Creating a Question Focus

Your student . . .	General Education Topics
• Is not turning in homework. • Is doing OK but could work harder. • Seems bored. • Is very strong in some areas, but weak in others. • Will need to attend summer school. • Needs additional help. • Is having some behavior problems. • Is falling behind classmates. • Is struggling in _____ (e.g., math, science, reading, writing).	• Report cards • Curriculum • Changes in schedule • School policies (attendance, discipline, class assignments, homework) • Testing • Parent-teacher partnership

up with these four rules. Now, if you've quickly done the math, you know that comes out to half a rule per year. We actually spent a good amount of time over all those years trying to figure out which of the 100 or so possible suggestions about how to ask your own questions could be eliminated. We tried to answer this question: *What is the absolute minimum number of rules needed in order to make it easier for all people to ask their own questions?*

Einstein said, "Make things as simple as possible and no simpler." The wisdom of that observation is relevant here. We would be delighted if there were a need for only one rule, specifically the first one: *Ask as many questions as you can.* However, we have learned through much trial and error that without the other three rules, the first one alone is not sufficient to get everyone asking their own questions. The other three rules create a safe space and a disciplined "no judgment" zone that encourages people to think and question freely without fear of being considered to have asked a "stupid question."

The four rules together create the safe environment within which even reticent parents can begin to identify what they don't know or what they want to know.

Produce the Questions

Following the rules, parents produce all kinds of questions without discussing, judging, or trying to answer them. They are also encouraged to number their questions in sequential order, which will make it easier to work on the next parts of the process.

Step 2: Improve Your Questions

Categorize the Questions

You will share with parents this simple definition of closed- and open-ended questions: Closed-ended questions can be answered with one word (e.g., *yes* or *no*). Open-ended questions require an explanation or more information. Parents then review their list of questions and categorize each one as closed or open.

This may appear to be a simple task, but it can be challenging at times and it can stimulate a lot of new thinking about questions and their structure.

Discuss the Value of Each Question Category

Parents are asked to name the advantages and disadvantages of asking each type of question. They learn that each type is useful based on purpose. This message may be contrary to the commonly held idea that some questions—the open-ended ones—are better than others.

Practice Changing Questions from One Category to the Other

Parents then practice changing questions from closed to open and from open to closed and gain a deeper understanding of question formulation. This exercise in categorizing and then changing their questions brings an important new awareness for parents. They often comment that they not only learned about the different kinds of questions and how to change them but also discovered through the process that "how you ask a question can get you different kinds of information."

Step 3: Prioritize Your Questions

Prioritization helps parents assess their own questions and prepares them for strategizing on their next steps. The discussion that occurs while prioritizing allows them to think more deeply about their questions.

Select Priority Questions Based on Prioritization Instructions

Parents choose three priority questions based on the prioritization instructions you will provide. Instructions will vary depending on specific goals, purposes, next steps, and many other factors. The design of the prioritization instructions should be part of a process for preparing to use the QFT. Examples include the following:

- Which three questions do you want to get answered first?
- Which three questions are the most important to you?
- Which three questions will help you address the problem immediately?
- Which three questions will help you figure out your next steps?

Step 4: Discuss and Strategize on Next Steps

Parents now are ready to work on their next steps, what they will do with their priority questions, and the insights they have gained through working with all of their questions. Next steps might be to gather new information, plan to meet with people who can or should be asked the questions, engage more parents and educators in thinking about the questions, or develop an action plan based on the questions. There are many avenues to explore, and selecting one will depend on the specific needs and purposes of each situation.

Step 5: Reflect on What Has Been Learned

Taking a moment for reflection may seem unnecessary at this point or, at best, a luxury that time does not allow. Parents have already done much of the intellectual labor, produced their own questions, refined their questions, prioritized them, and strategized on how to use them as they weigh next steps. They have done a lot. Why, then, is it important to now add a few minutes for them to reflect on such basic questions as "What did you learn?" and "How can you use it?"

These kinds of simple reflection questions stimulate a deeper awareness of what they, themselves, have discovered by doing all of this hard intellectual labor. They realize that they have not only done a lot of work but also learned a great deal "just" by working in a rigorous way with their own questions. They are thinking about their thinking. This helps reinforce all that they learned and allows them to see themselves as fully capable. Even though they are neither the professionals nor the experts, they are fully capable of engaging in a thinking process on an important subject. The small investment of time at the end of the process—even just 3–5 minutes—can greatly amplify the value of all that came before.

Changes after Going through the QFT Process

Going through the QFT process can be a transformational experience, influencing what parents know, how they feel, and what they are ready and able to do.

- *Cognitive:* Parents now know how to produce their own questions. They have a process and structure for doing it. They know four rules that help them do that. They know about open- and closed-ended questions and what happens when you change them. They know how to prioritize using specific criteria and instructions. They know how to use their priority questions to strategize and determine next steps.

- *Affective:* Parents feel better about their own intellectual abilities. They become more confident, moving from a sense of powerlessness—of "not even knowing what to ask"—to a sense of their own capability to think, ask questions, and speak up. The thinking process and identification of priority questions and next steps also generates a new sense of urgency to take action, play a role in their children's education, and partner with their children's educators. They also feel that they have a license to ask questions—permission they can grant themselves.
- *Behavioral:* Parents ask questions. They work with their questions. They prioritize. They strategize. They take informed action. They participate more. Teachers regularly report that they have the best and most productive meetings with parents who have learned to use the Question Formulation Technique.

Building these three thinking abilities and producing the cognitive, affective, and behavioral changes does not require hours and hours or multiple meetings or sessions. There's no need to learn to teach a lengthy curriculum. You can facilitate a quick version of the entire QFT process in as little as 10 minutes with individual parents and in about 30 minutes with groups of parents. It would be better to have more time, even up to an hour for a workshop-type event with a group of parents, but that's not absolutely necessary.

The Framework for Accountable Decision Making (FADM)

The Framework for Accountable Decision Making (FADM), one of the three core components of the Right Question Strategy, is a useful resource that can be used on its own. You will see, however, that when parents use it in combination with the QFT, they can become even more effective participants in their children's education. Just as the QFT builds sophisticated thinking abilities in a simple and rigorous manner, so does the FADM provide parents with a simple structure that makes it easier to understand and participate more effectively in critically important decisions that affect their children. It does this with just three parts:

- A simple and clear definition of a decision that then makes it easier for parents to clearly identify key decisions affecting their children.
- Three specific criteria for analyzing a decision. Parents need to be able to focus sharply on the basis for making the decision, the process for making it, and their role in the process.
- Use of the three criteria as a focus for asking questions. Parents can apply their question-asking skill with a sharp focus on the most important aspects of each decision.

Step 1: Define and Identify Decisions

The FADM begins with a two-part introduction to decisions:

- *Defining the term* decision: A decision is the selection of one option from among two or more options. The apparent simplicity of this definition should not detract from its importance. For many parents, there is a catalytic effect to discovering that a decision is not always a done deal but rather the result of choosing between different options. This new knowledge presents an opportunity to examine all options more closely and to inquire about the option that has been or will ultimately be selected.
- *Identifying decisions:* A definition of a decision is just a starting point for looking at decisions. Even armed with a clear definition, it can sometimes be surprisingly difficult to even recognize decisions that are being made. Parents might find out about new classroom assignments, changes in homework practices, and new disciplinary practices without realizing that each new topic presented to them is actually the result of a decision; that is, it was the option chosen. There are specific resources in

Appendix B that scaffold a learning process that allows parents to identify many decisions they make each day—how a decision about what to eat or wear or how to get to an appointment—are all the selection of one option from among two or more options. This awareness of their own decision-making expertise can then build confidence for examining decisions beginning at the classroom or school level.

Step 2: Explore Three Key Elements in Decision Making

Parents are introduced to criteria for good decision making. This includes the following key information they should look for in any decision that affects their children:

- *Reason:* the basis for the decisions. Decisions must be based on policies, standards, and rules that are fairly applied. Decisions should be legitimate. Zeroing in on the reason for a decision can help clarify why one particular option was selected (sometimes, there are multiple reasons for a decision, but there must always be at least one reason). Parents often report that even though they may not agree with a decision, or they may not get the outcome they want, knowing the reason and getting an explanation for the decision helps them understand the perspective of their children's educators. Making clear that they expect to know a reason also makes clear that decision makers are accountable to the people affected by the decision.
- *Process:* all that goes into selecting the option and making the decision. Fully knowing about the process requires learning about the information used, the steps leading up to the selection of one option, who was (and was not) involved, and the logistics of when and where the decision was made. An accountable decision requires transparency. The people affected by the decision need to know *how* the decision was made. By learning about the

process, parents often discover the complexity of the decision making process, how many people need to be involved, and the many factors that must be considered.

- *Role:* the part a parent can play in the decision-making process. In an accountable decision-making process, it is not sufficient to know just about the reasons for a decision and the process for making it. Those criteria are necessary but not sufficient. It is also important to find a way to have a say, to play some kind of role in the process. This does not mean that the parent is the decision maker or has veto power. It does mean that at some point in the process, the parent can and should play a role in decisions affecting a child's education. This could be early in a process, inviting full participation. It could be late in the process to share results of initial work and planning and to discuss possible options. Alternatively, it could even be at the end of a process with clear information about how to appeal or change a decision. Parents who are consulted early and often understand more, are more likely to feel their voices are heard, and have a greater understanding of the complex factors that go into any one particular decision affecting their children.

Step 3: Ask Questions about Decisions

What, then, is the most direct way to learn about the reason for a decision, the process for making it, and the role a parent can play? Ask questions and deliberately use these three criteria to inform one's own questions. It is important to be able to ask questions about all three, for altogether they represent three fundamental democratic decision-making principles:

- Reason is related to Legitimacy.
- Process is related to Transparency.
- Role is related to Opportunities for Participation.

Accountable decision making, at any level in a democratic society, must meet all three criteria. Parents who ask questions about a reason but are not prepared to ask about the process—about how the decisions are made—are less prepared to advocate for their children and partner effectively with educators. The same is true for parents who ask about the process or reason for making a decision but fail to ask about the role they could or should play in the decision. Parents who ask questions about all three are well-equipped partners for educators who want to improve outcomes for all children in their school.

When parents combine the Framework for Accountable Decision Making (FADM) with the Question Formulation Technique (QFT), they are well equipped to partner effectively with their children's educators. They can more easily and confidently move from being passive bystanders to active, strategic participants in decisions. The FADM, similar to the QFT, produces distinct cognitive, affective, and behavioral changes.

- *Cognitive:* Parents gain new knowledge of a simple definition of a decision. They know how to discern decisions from general topics and issues. They know the meaning of three specific criteria for accountable decision making. They know how to create questions that address all three criteria.
- *Affective:* Informed by this new knowledge, parents feel more confident participating in decisions, asking questions, and exploring how they can play a role in decision making. Realizing the complexity of the decision-making process can produce both new feelings of empathy for the challenges facing educators and a greater sense of urgency to make sure their own voices on behalf of their children are heard.
- *Behavioral:* Parents pay attention to decisions, monitor decision making at multiple levels, ask questions about decisions, use the criteria for accountable decision making when asking questions,

participate in decision making, and partner more effectively with their children's educators.

Parents who are able to do all of this also become strong community partners and effective advocates on behalf of their children's schools and educators. From the individual to the community to the district to the state, parents who can participate in decisions and ask good questions are an invaluable resource for all schools.

The Support, Monitor, and Advocate Model

We learned a great deal from the parents with whom we worked when they began using their enhanced skills for asking questions and participating in decisions. They were the source for highlighting the importance of asking questions, and they also helped us learn about the significance of applying the skill of question formulation to participating effectively in decisions. As we observed them move into action, we learned about how they were able to partner most effectively with their children's educators when they played three distinct roles.

Support

Parents best support their children's education when they try, as best they can, to meet their children's basic health, nutritional, and emotional needs. They also communicate clearly to their children that they consider education a priority, create space and time for students to do schoolwork at home, and do the best they can to ensure students arrive safely to school and return safely to home.

Monitor

Parents who effectively monitor their children's education begin to ask more questions about how their children are faring in school, if they are making appropriate academic progress, and whether they feel safe and comfortable in the school environment. They check in with their children, pay attention to homework assignments, review and exchange communication with the teacher and school, and take note of how their children are performing on tests and the grades they are getting.

Advocate

Sometimes, the heightened level of parent action—actively supporting and monitoring their children's education—is not sufficient to meet their children's needs. Parents who are actively monitoring might notice a decline in student performance, a sudden reluctance to go to school, or a more negative attitude toward school. Parents who notice this begin to use their question-asking skills to talk to the teacher and communicate with the school about the changes they have observed. Because they have been carefully monitoring how their children were doing and were able to notice a change, their advocacy means a lot—not only for their children but also for the school. Parents are an invaluable set of eyes and ears to keep tabs on how an individual student is doing. In classrooms with more than 30 students and schools with more than 1,000 students, it is hard for educators to stay on top of everything. Parents who can advocate for their children become partners in working to ensure student success.

The Value of a Simple Model for Effective Parent Action

The challenges in education are so great, in fact, that parents are sometimes blamed for all that they are not doing on behalf of their children's education. There is much that is demanded of them. Parents may be handed a daunting laundry list of all of the things they should be doing to support their children's education. Inadvertently, such well-intentioned sharing of information actually places additional pressure on parents who struggle every day to meet the health and welfare needs of their children. Juggling jobs, working two shifts, searching for employment, struggling with health issues, or dealing with transportation challenges and safety concerns, parents already have a lot on their plate. Expecting them to get far more involved in their children's education and check off a long list of suggested actions can have the opposite effect. Parents who are overwhelmed by a range of challenges may retreat from any involvement in education, trusting or simply leaving the job of educating their children to the professionals.

The parents with whom we have worked in many communities around the country have created and modeled a simpler pathway to effective partnership with their children's educators. Their actions should be recognized as a model because that will make it easier for others to emulate. The Support, Monitor, and Advocate Model is both simple and fundamentally important at the same time. Effective partnership is far more likely when parents are confident that they can play three specific roles: support their children's education, monitor their progress, and advocate for them when necessary.

We value and respect their initiative. Describing their actions as a model—the Support, Monitor, and Advocate Model for effective parent action—simplifies and demystifies what they actually need to do to help their children. They appreciate how the model makes it easier for them to focus sharply on just three key roles and allows them to name their actions as part of a larger effort to create a more effective partnership.

The Support, Monitor, and Advocate Model—as the third core component of the Right Question School-Family Partnership Strategy—is consistent with the simplicity and depth of both the Question Formulation Technique and the Framework for Accountable Decision Making. In the chapters to come, you will have the opportunity to learn how educators and parents have used the three components of the Right Question Strategy to build strong, lasting, and meaningful partnerships.

2 Partnership Through Teacher-Initiated Change

The Problem

The achievement disparities that manifest themselves so vividly in high school dropout rates and lack of readiness for higher education can begin early in a child's educational experience. Here's a familiar challenge: a teacher notices that one student has not turned in his homework several times over the past few weeks. Is it because he didn't do it? Does he forget to bring it in? Is there anything else going on? Is he resisting the assignments because he is having trouble with the content? Are there issues at home that make it difficult for him to do his homework? All of these questions, from the initial closed-ended ones to a larger open-ended question of *why* can flash through a teacher's mind in a matter of seconds. She's seen the problem before and without even consciously starting a list, she can rapidly name a wide range of possible causes.

Often, a student shows a few signs of struggling, but the problem does not rise to the level of a crisis. Thus, the student, as well as his teacher, keep muddling through. The teacher—her hands full working with 20–30 other students, two of whom are usually disrupting the class nearly every day—has to assess whether the concern requires immediate action. The parent, not hearing about any serious problem, is relieved that her child does not need to be at the top of her worry list.

When does this relatively minor concern become a more serious problem? When does not responding to a smaller problem create more problems later on? What bad things need to happen to make this seemingly insignificant matter a priority?

What can the teacher do? The options are limited. She can start by having a conversation with the student about why he's not bringing in his homework. If that doesn't help, she may move to imposing more severe consequences with the hope that the fear of a lower grade or lack of access to a desired activity might cause the behavior to change. Is there a need to bring in a counselor? Might this be a sign of special needs or particular difficulties that can only be addressed with an Individualized Education Program (IEP)? It feels too early in the process to jump to that conclusion.

Seeking a Partner: Traditional Forms of Communication with Parents

The teacher needs and deserves a family partner in addressing the problem and invites the student's parent to meet. What is the likelihood that such a meeting will happen? This child's parent, a single mother with two other children in the house, has never before initiated contact with the teacher and has only sporadically and reluctantly responded to any outreach efforts from the school.

For many parents, this relatively small problem can feel like a crisis well beyond their control, pushing them into uncomfortable terrain. An invitation to meet with the teacher, especially about a problem their child is having, can provoke embarrassment, fear, insecurity, and inadequacy—all influenced and sometimes compounded by problems older siblings or parents themselves have experienced. Some parents may react by "fleeing" from a conversation with the teacher; alternatively, some may express an emotional "fight" response, blaming the teacher or school, which leads to greater frustration and lower morale.

In the meantime, the teacher has a lot on her plate and not enough time to get it all done. Nevertheless, she has still made efforts to connect with parents; she has given them her contact information, shared periodic updates through the school website and newsletter, and requested their daily sign-off on homework. She has also made a point to follow up promptly with parents' requests for information, to invite them to meetings, and to check in with parents routinely (but especially when there is an issue to address). The school administration, recognizing the need to engage parents as partners, has also communicated key information to families and has encouraged teachers to use some "best practices" in parent outreach. They have sent welcome letters with instructions for accessing the school website and grading website, and they have given parents advice for how to engage in their children's learning from home, such as tips for talking to their children about what they're learning, the importance of routines and organized work spaces, and tips for making lists of questions to ask their children's teachers.

So what's wrong with communicating information to parents in these ways? Nothing. It makes sense to give parents such information, and it may be very helpful for some parents. One-way communication, however, has limited value even when it is inviting communication in return.

For example, what does the parent really get from some advice about "setting aside homework space"? It depends. Some assumptions are built into all of these efforts to communicate with parents— that they understand the importance of the homework and why their children are doing homework in the first place (aside from because it's what is expected). It seems like an obvious thing to assume, but knowing that homework is expected of students is not the same thing as understanding how the homework connects to what the teacher is teaching, helps the student keep up with the class, and allows the teacher to assess understanding.

Frustrated, the teacher is unsure about what else to do. She finds the list of questions the school gave out to all parents and considers sending the questions about homework to all parents as a reminder, hoping they will trigger more awareness among parents about the importance of the homework.

What's wrong with giving parents the questions to ask? Again, on the face of it, nothing. Questions are important, and professionals can help identify the most important questions to ask. Handing a list of questions to parents, however, can also reinforce a message that their role is to "receive" information. It communicates the unintended message that "we know better than you what questions to ask," and the parent stays dependent on educators to ask questions about issues that they don't understand well.

Building Parent Skills to Ask Questions and Problem Solve

What could dramatically change the dynamic for this teacher, who is now left on her own to try to solve this problem? What if the child's mother could be a real partner with the teacher? What would that look like? How could the teacher help build that partnership, knowing all too well that a simple invitation to meet about a "problem" could provoke all sorts of negative feelings and reactions from the parent?

What if, presented with this specific concern, the parent could ask her own set of questions, probe with the teacher about the causes of the problem, and explore solutions? How would that change the dynamic?

In order to build a stronger partnership, parents need to know how to produce their own questions. They also need to work with their own questions and learn how to improve their questions. They may be different or just differently worded than the educators' questions, but parents will be better prepared to set a learning and problem-solving agenda if they are the ones coming up with questions.

It is hard to fully grasp, at first, that such a seemingly simple action—a mother asking questions about her child's schoolwork—could significantly change the dynamic, create a partnership with the teacher, and improve outcomes for her child. It becomes clearer when we look more closely at what changes.

Imagine the parent coming in and being asked to respond to the teacher's well-intentioned questions. Even the simple ones that first flashed through the teacher's mind can often come across as an unwelcome cross-examination that puts the parent on the defensive. Great power resides in the person asking the question: the more knowledgeable participant often asks the questions, and the less knowledgeable participant's role is to respond. However, if the teacher presents the problem as one to be solved together, then she has created a new opening to build an equal partnership. The focus shifts solely from what the teacher wants to know to a broader conversation so that *the parent can set a learning agenda that becomes part of a problem-solving agenda.*

This is the fundamental difference in moving toward helping parents learn to ask their own questions about challenges their children are facing at school. In almost every setting in which a professional is working with a layperson—a doctor with a patient, a lawyer with a client, or a teacher with a parent—the power of the question usually resides in the hands of the professional. Wielded effectively by the professional, this powerful tool can, of course, lead to productive results.

What changes when the layperson is able to wield the same tool? He or she discovers, as the professionals already know, that there is no more powerful tool for problem solving than the ability to ask one's own questions. Peter Drucker (1954), the 20th century business strategist who created the field of management consulting, believed that the key to successful practice of management was to ask the right questions—because an abundance of answers already exists. Drucker's insight helped create a multibillion dollar industry of management consulting firms that are paid large amounts of money "just" because they know how to ask the right questions.

Drucker's analysis, and the highly educated and highly paid consultants, might make it even more difficult to imagine the mother of this young boy figuring out "the right questions" to ask in order to partner with the teacher to solve the problem. But she can learn to do that, and when she does, it can make all the difference. She would not be dependent on a consultant or anyone else to help her support her child's education, monitor his progress, advocate for him, and partner with the teacher.

The QFT as a Resource for Learning to Ask Better Questions

The Question Formulation Technique is designed not to supplant existing efforts but to complement and enhance them. It is a foundational strategy for building partnerships with families. Skip over that foundation and the many other well-intentioned efforts may not have much of an impact. Build the foundation, however, and the partnership can grow. The QFT is a resource for building that foundation because it helps parents learn to (1) produce their own questions, (2) improve their own questions, and (3) strategize using their questions. These are three distinct steps, each one a model of rigorous thinking.

This is no small matter. Imagine parents asking a wide range of high-quality questions and brainstorming with the teacher about the role of homework in their children's education. Such a dynamic discussion is likely to bring about some positive changes. The parent moves from silent outsider to inquisitive participant in an information-gathering process. When the parent starts working on her questions, she does more than simply prepare some questions. She's finding out lots of essential details, such as what the teacher has observed, how many times this behavior has happened, what her son says, and what the teacher has tried to do. The parent then moves on to form a part of the solution, asking questions about what can be done to address the problem and her own role in the solution. Finally, the parent works with the teacher to determine action steps toward the solution. This way, the parent is not passively waiting to hear from the teacher but rather figuring out how to play a more proactive role. The process starts with looking at what can be done at home that would be helpful, but it does not end there. The questions can move to expectations that the teacher and other school staff will help set and monitor for the student so as to manage and address any future problems that emerge.

These categories of questions are all forms of action: gathering information, monitoring performance, and taking action. Indeed, they are not just important forms of action, they are directly relevant not only to solving the immediate problem but also to ensure greater success over the long haul. A parent who learns to do this early in the year is a partner throughout the year. A parent who learns to do this early in a child's school experience is a partner throughout the years of schooling.

A partnership in which a parent is asking questions and problem solving with the teacher is rare in many communities. It's so rare, in fact, that it may seem too difficult for overburdened schools and overwhelmed teachers to create on their own. They need and deserve a resource they can easily implement to help build a true partnership.

Observing the Question Formulation Technique in Action

In the following scenario, you'll see how the Question Formulation Technique is used by one teacher and one parent to help create a partnership to address a student's struggles with doing his homework.

You will see the core components of the Question Formulation Technique that were described in full in the Introduction. They include the following steps:

- The teacher, on her own, sets a goal for working with the parent and designs a Question Focus (a focus for the parent's questions).
- The teacher explains that she wants to work with the parent to come up with some questions to help them both look at what they can do.
- The teacher informally shares with the parent the Rules for Producing Questions.
- The parent produces questions.
- The teacher works with the parent to recognize the differences between open- and closed-ended questions, and the parent discusses advantages and disadvantages of asking both types of questions.
- The parent looks at the list of questions, identifies open- and closed-ended questions, and changes a couple of them.
- The parent prioritizes questions she wants to address.

- The parent and teacher work on an action plan.
- The parent reflects on what she has learned.

Case Study: Tackling Homework Problems

Identifying the Problem

About a month into the new academic year, Ms. T noticed that S was often not turning in his homework. It took her by surprise because S seemed to have made the transition to 3rd grade fairly well and hadn't presented any problems in class. Unbeknownst to S's mother, S's 2nd grade teacher had talked with the assistant principal about possibly getting S tested for special education services. However, several other students in the class had more pressing needs and were more disruptive, so S had just moved through the year without any seemingly major problems or consequent intervention. Ms. T, in preparation for the new year, had reviewed notes on all of the students, learned about the 2nd grade teacher's recommendation for a referral, and was on the alert for any challenges S might present in her classroom. She was satisfied with S's progress and saw no need to worry—that is, until he surprised her by not doing his homework for the third time in the past two weeks.

Ms. T had seen similar challenges before in her 10 years in the classroom. She had actually instituted a policy of telling students that they needed a parent at home to initial their homework when it was done. She also was aware that that policy sometimes created difficult interactions at home, either because a student was reluctant to reveal he or she couldn't complete the homework or because a parent was uncomfortable with signing off on something unfamiliar. Ms. T didn't want to escalate problems, so she often stopped insisting on a parental sign-off.

Instead, she began to address the problem by talking with the student; if that didn't work, she moved on to sending a note home alerting the parent(s) of the concern. Sometimes, she was hesitant to do so because she didn't want to unnecessarily alarm the parents. She knew most of her students' parents were under enough stress. Some worked late hours, some pieced together two or three part-time jobs, and some were looking for work. Their lives were full of challenges, and she didn't want to add to them. She didn't want to add to the students' stress, either, by putting them at risk of a stern rebuke when there may not be a justification for it.

Still, she pushed ahead and sent notes home. In response to the notes, parents tended either not to respond at all or to nod quietly through a meeting in deference to Ms. T, promising that their child wouldn't cause any problems. Once in a while, parents would show up defensive, critical, and upset—influenced, in part, from bad experiences with older siblings or their own negative memories from school.

In the case of S, Ms. T had talked to him and that didn't seem to change anything. She sent notes home, with no response, and report cards and parent-teacher conferences were still several weeks away. She was very concerned that S was at risk of falling behind if no action was taken.

A New Solution

She thought about sending home the list of recommended questions the school came up with about what parents could ask about homework. But, she rarely heard those questions from parents and didn't think that sending a list would be effective. Her classroom practice had also influenced her thinking about that as she had moved from giving students research questions to answer to help them formulate their own questions. This got her thinking more.

Ms. T was an active user of Twitter and used it occasionally to join in national conversations about education. She was a quiet leader. She was an "early adopter" of ideas that could improve her teaching, and she liked the feeling of working in her own classroom but also being part of a larger group of educators who were looking for ideas that could help their students learn.

She suddenly remembered a recent Twitter chat she had participated in about different ways schools are using the Question Formulation Technique (QFT) in their classrooms. The Twitter chat attracted educators from around the country. One teacher shared how he had used the QFT to help parents come prepared with their own questions for parent-teacher conferences. Another light bulb went off for Ms. T: "That's what I should try with parents, especially when there's a problem I need their help with."

Ms. T was intrigued by using the QFT with adults, both in faculty meetings as some had done and with parents. She was already experienced and comfortable using the QFT for teaching and learning purposes and had been excited especially by how her students felt that "when you ask the question, you feel like it's your job to get the answer." She loved seeing that sense of ownership and saw how it actually made her job a good bit easier. It reinforced the message she got when initially introduced to the QFT by one of the instructional coaches in her district solely for the purpose of helping students become better problem solvers in math. "You'll feel some of that teaching thrill that comes when the light bulbs go off, but now it won't be happening just for those kids who are always quick to get something. You'll see it come from surprising places, especially from kids who often shut down when being introduced to something new. The QFT actually honors not knowing, so there's new space for them to ask questions rather than to have to name what they know. When those light bulbs come on, you'll feel some joy you deserve!"

Something about the idea of using the QFT with parents rang true for her, given her past experiences with sending worrisome notes home. She liked the idea of starting with seeing parents as great assets for any effort to help a student do well in school. It was an extension of how she liked working with her students and thinking about their strengths—the ways in which they were intelligent—rather than focusing on everything they didn't know or couldn't do. She decided to give it a shot!

She was ready to try it, but she wondered if she could easily make the change to using the QFT with parents. After all, she still had 24 kids other than S to worry about, she had 25 kids to teach the following day, and the principal had a meeting with all teachers about the schoolwide commitment to test prep for the next day.

Goals in Using the Question Formulation Technique

Ms. T was familiar with the planning process for effectively using the QFT and knew just how to begin. She started preparing her work with S's mother, Ms. P, by outlining some specific outcomes she hoped to achieve:

- Ms. P becomes aware of the problem.
- Ms. P learns and feels more comfortable playing a role in S's education.
- Ms. P partners and communicates with Ms. T to help solve the problem.
- S begins to do his homework and has more success in school.

Ms. T knew she needed to list a few options for her Question Focus design, looking critically at each one rather than getting stuck on the first one that came to mind. She tried to keep in mind one of the key criteria for an effective Question Focus: simplicity. She came up with the following:

1. S is not doing his homework.
2. Something seems to have changed about S.
3. Three times in the past two weeks, S didn't turn his homework in.
4. S seems to be having trouble doing his homework.
5. S is struggling with lessons when he doesn't do his homework.

6. Anytime he has trouble with something in class, S doesn't do the homework I assign.

She reviewed the options and assessed them:

1. S is not doing his homework. *True statement but just sounds the alarm without any cushion. May provoke panic.*

2. Something seems to have changed about S. *True statement but worrisome and may set off a fearful emotional reaction, blocking thinking.*

3. Three times in the past two weeks, S didn't turn his homework in. *Specific, factual, time bound so could prevent perceiving him as "never" working.*

4. S seems to be having trouble doing his homework. *Suggesting a concern, opening up to exploration, particularly ripe for helping to create some safe space for asking questions.*

5. S is struggling with lessons when he doesn't do his homework. *Teacher's analysis of implications of not doing homework. Might overwhelm parent in starting off the conversation, inviting questions about a topic that the teacher knows much better than the parent—how the homework is connected to classwork.*

6. Anytime he has trouble with something in class, he doesn't do the homework I assign. *Could be overwhelming also.*

The Meeting

Ms. T studied her Question Focus ideas and tried to think about which would lead to a productive line of questioning to more easily bring Ms. P into the conversation. She decided on Question Focus 4; *S seems to be having trouble doing his homework.* That evening, she called Ms. P, and after a few words about how much she enjoys having S in her class, she told Ms. P that she would really like to meet with her to talk about how they can work together to help S do well in school. It was not easy for Ms. P to schedule a meeting around her job and responsibilities with her other children, but she made the time to come in.

Ms. T welcomed Ms. P and told her again how much she likes having S in her class and pointed to a couple of specific examples of good work that S had done, which Ms. P was pleased to hear. Then Ms. T explained that she's been concerned the last few weeks about S's work and wanted to see how they both could help him.

"I'd like to think about this with you in a way that I've learned is a really good way to figure things out, a way to think about things that might be different or difficult. I've used it now a lot in class and it's been really good. Would that be OK?"

Ms. P didn't feel like she was in a position to say no, but she also liked how Ms. T described the idea. It made her feel more comfortable.

Introducing the Question Formulation Technique

Ms. T said that she wanted Ms. P's help in thinking about how S could do better in school. She would like them to work together and start by asking some questions about how to help him rather than just talk about it. "This is a kind of shortcut to figuring out what we can both do. We just need to try to ask any questions that come to mind—as many as we can without stopping to talk about or answer any of them right away."

Ms. P didn't show much of a reaction, so Ms. T added, "This felt a little different the first time I did it, but it really helps and we'll get to working on the answers soon."

She then presented the Question Focus: "Here's what we'll be asking about: *S seems to be having trouble doing his homework.*"

Silence. Ms. P was waiting for Ms. T to go first. Ms. T said, "What questions come to mind when you hear that?"

Ms. P started slowly. "What do you mean?" fully expecting Ms. T to answer that question, but Ms. T said, "Well, we won't stop to talk about one question right now, so let's list a few. What do you want to ask?"

Ms. T looked perplexed but then asked, "Is he behaving? Is he causing problems?"

Aware that disruptive behavior is often parents' primary concern when they hear about a challenge for their children, Ms. T felt a need to say, "Well, I don't want to stop you, but I don't want you to worry about that. I'm not worried about his behavior."

This was important. Ms. P relaxed, even smiled. Ms. T wrote down Ms. P's first two questions as Ms. P had worded them and repeated the QFocus: *S seems to be having trouble doing his homework.*

"What other questions do you have?" Ms. T asked.

Now that the fear that S was misbehaving had been put aside, Ms. P quickly came up with a few questions:

- Is he doing his homework?
- What do you mean by "trouble"?
- How do you know he's having trouble?

Ms. T kept writing the questions, exactly as Ms. P had put them. She slowed down and was silent for a moment. Ms. T didn't jump in; she trusts the process, and her patience in waiting for more questions was a sign of respect for Ms. P.

Ms. P then sat up straight: "When did this start? Did he do his homework before?"

As Ms. P was asking her questions, Ms. T realized that the questions were actually helping her analyze the problem more closely. Ms. P's questions got her thinking about whether there was a specific moment—perhaps when they began to do more math homework as they were preparing for the state tests—when S stopped turning in his homework.

Ms. P noticed that change in Ms. T and asked her whether these questions were what she was looking for.

"Oh," Ms. T said, "they're helping me think about this. Let's try to see if there are any others you want to ask."

Ms. P's questions turned to consequences:

- Is he getting punished for not doing his homework?
- What's going to happen to him?

Then, after another pause, she asked, "Why do you think he's having trouble?"

She seemed to fully expect an immediate answer, again seeing the teacher as the more knowledgeable one. Ms. T didn't want to be the only one thinking about possible reasons, so she said, "Well, let's hold off on answering any of these questions. Are there any others you want to ask?"

Ms. P then quietly asked, "What should I do to make sure he does his homework?"

Ms. T did her best to hold herself back from exclaiming, "Great question!" because she knew that judging a question, even positively, might suggest that other questions were not as good. This question, of course, is the foundation for building a partnership. Instead of being told what to do or getting an information packet about what she could do to help, Ms. P had just established a learning agenda for herself. She asked the question. She was now more interested in getting an answer.

Ms. T invited Ms. P to look at their list of questions. "Wow, this is quite a list!" she said, now comfortably being able to acknowledge the good work Ms. P had done. "One thing I've learned is to look at the difference between questions that can be answered with a simple *yes* or *no* and questions that require more explanation. Let's first look and see which *yes* or *no* questions, also called 'closed-ended questions,' are on the list."

1. Is he behaving?
2. Is he causing problems?
3. Is he doing his homework?
4. What do you mean by "trouble"?
5. How do you know he's having trouble?
6. When did this start?
7. Did he do his homework before?
8. Is he getting punished for not doing his homework?

9. What's going to happen to him?

10. Why do you think he's having trouble?

11. What should I do to make sure he does his homework?

Ms. P looked at the first question and hesitantly said, "Well, I do want to know, just *yes* or *no*, if he's behaving, so I guess it is one of those questions, a closed question." She put a *C* by it. Then she got more confident labeling questions 2 and 3 as closed-ended. She paused at question 4, "What do you mean by 'trouble?'" saying, "I do want to know what you mean by that. But that's not *yes* or *no*."

Ms. T explained, "Those kinds of questions that require more explanation are called open-ended questions. What do you think about number 4?"

Ms. P was clear that question 4 was indeed open-ended, and she put an *O* next to it and then did the same with question 5. Question 6 was closed-ended, so she wrote a C beside it.

1. Is he behaving? C

2. Is he causing problems? C

3. Is he doing his homework? C

4. What do you mean by "trouble"? O

5. How do you know he's having trouble? O

6. When did this start? C

She paused when looking at question 7—"Did he do his homework before?"—and was not sure. She wondered if there were a quick answer and whether that would make it a closed-ended question. Ms. T didn't want her to worry about whether the labels were all correct. She was more interested in getting Ms. P into the thinking process, so she suggested, "How about if we say that could go either way?" and marked it *O/C*.

They then went quickly through the rest of the list, and Ms. P seemed to be enjoying confidently labeling the questions.

7. Did he do his homework before? O/C

8. Is he getting punished for not doing his homework? C
9. What's going to happen to him? O
10. Why do you think he's having trouble? O
11. What should I do to make sure he does his homework? O

It had taken about 7 minutes to get to this point, and Ms. T wanted to make sure Ms. P had a chance to try to change any of the questions and then get to the key next step: prioritizing the questions. She then asked Ms. P to look at her questions and choose a closed one she wanted to change to open and vice versa.

Ms. P was not quite sure about this step and was silent. Ms. T said, "Well, look at question 8, 'Is he getting punished for not doing his homework?' What else do you want to know?"

Ms. P was quick with a new question: "What happens when he doesn't do his homework?"

She then moved on to change an open-ended question to a closed-ended one. She looked at question 9 and changed the open-ended "What's going to happen to him?" to a closed one that voiced a great but unspoken fear: "Will he be held back?"

1. Is he behaving?
2. Is he causing problems?
3. Is he doing his homework?
4. What do you mean by "trouble?"
5. How do you know he's having trouble?
6. When did this start?
7. Did he do his homework before?
8. Is he getting punished for not doing his homework?
9. What's going to happen to him?
10. Why do you think he's having trouble?
11. What should I do to make sure he does his homework?
12. What happens when he doesn't do his homework? (changed from question 8)
13. Will he be held back? (changed from question 9)

Ms. T showed Ms. P that she had 13 questions now and said, "Let's do one more thing here. Which do you think are the three most important questions?"

Ms. P wasn't sure quite how to think about that. Question 1 was very important to her—"Is he behaving?"—but she knew by this point that they were really trying to work on the homework problem, so she went further down the list. She marked these questions:

5. How do you know he's having trouble?
7. Did he do his homework before?
9. What's going to happen to him?
10. Why do you think he's having trouble?
11. What should I do to make sure he does his homework?
13. Will he be held back?

These questions made it clear to Ms. T how much Ms. P is worried about consequences and her son starting down a slippery slope to more serious outcomes such as being held back. She was having trouble prioritizing. Ms. T, aware that the prioritization step can be a challenge to do on one's own, narrowed the criteria a bit to get Ms. P from worrying about consequences to focusing more on this task. "Well, what do you think we should focus on to help him do better?"

This sharpened the prioritization process quite a bit, and Ms. P chose questions 10, 11, and 13.

Priority Questions

10. Why do you think he's having trouble?
11. What should I do to make sure he does his homework?
13. Will he be held back?

Ms. T asked why she chose those three, and Ms. P replied, "I want to hear from you about what you think. And I want to know what I can do to help. And I'm really scared that he might be held back. I know how bad that would be."

It was very helpful to Ms. T to hear what Ms. P was most afraid of, her questions wanting to know more about why S might be having trouble, and, most significant of all, how she could play a role in helping solve the problem.

A Simple Plan to Solve the Problem

They spent some time looking at Ms. P's priority questions, and Ms. T felt comfortable addressing them. She was surprised by how quickly that part of the conversation went. She told Ms. P that her question "When did this start?" (question 6) helped her think about S's situation differently, and she realized the challenge began when she started assigning more math homework. It got her thinking about how to help S more effectively. Imagining what she could do, too, Ms. P was now more than ready to keep an eye on S's homework.

Quickly, they agreed to a plan—a simple one. They would inform S that his mother would expect to see his homework every time and would initial it once he completed it. Ms. T would be looking for that. If for some reason S didn't do his homework, he still needed his mother to initial it. If the reason for not doing it was because he felt that he couldn't do it or didn't understand it, then Ms. T would help him in the areas he was struggling with.

It was not an onerous plan. It didn't include a long list of things a parent had to do or lectures about setting aside a dedicated space or time for homework. Those suggestions could be part of a plan, for sure, but that was something Ms. P could decide on her own. Once they had the plan, Ms. P shared with Ms. T, "You know, I can use what I learned here to help my other kids, too. Now that I think about it, I can use this to help myself." Ms. T was excited about the applications Ms. P saw. She had planned to share some materials at the end of the meeting to help Ms. P prepare questions, and she knew now that these would be put to good use.

They had worked together to create a simple plan that allowed the parent to monitor the work that was being done and allowed the teacher both to monitor the work and to gain knowledge about what extra help the student needed.

Ms. T finished the QFT process by asking Ms. P to share what she liked about the process. When she uses the QFT with her students, she usually begins by asking, "What did you learn?" to help them reflect on the process. Here, she was establishing a connection with Ms. P and wanted to give her a chance to share her feelings.

Smiling again, Ms. P said, "It felt strange at first, but I really liked just coming up with these questions. It was different, and it helped me feel like I want to know more about what's happening with him."

Ms. T had hoped this feeling would come out of the process. It's a different starting point for building a partnership when the parent has a clear learning agenda. She then said the same thing she says to her students before one final question: "You came up with all of these questions, looked at closed- and open-ended questions, changed some of them, and then chose the most important ones for you. What did you learn?"

"I learned that the way you ask a question can get you different information," Ms. P said. "I never thought about that before. I also learned that it's really good to spend some time thinking about questions. I feel like now I know what I want to know. It's like if I spend some time on questions, I can actually come up with better questions to ask. I never knew that before."

All of this had happened in about 20 minutes. Ms. T had told Ms. P to plan on meeting for 45 minutes. These 20 minutes of focusing on questions "didn't feel like a detour," Ms. T thought, "but more like a shortcut." They could now get down to working together about what they each could do at school and at home to help S.

What Just Happened Here? A Lot!

For Ms. T, the use of the Question Formulation Technique created a very different starting point for a conversation with a parent about a struggling student. It didn't entirely solve the problem, but it did, however, create a different teacher-parent relationship. Ms. T felt like she was talking with a parent who was asking questions about the causes of a problem, consequences, concerns, ideas for how to address the problem, and—most strongly—ways the parent could help. Ms. T no longer felt alone in facing this challenge. Because Ms. P was brought into the process and came up with questions that were important to her, she now had her own learning agenda and felt more prepared for the next stage: looking at specific things they both could do.

The strategy they adopted built on Ms. T's intent at the beginning of the year to ask parents to initial students' homework. Now, however, that request had a completely different meaning for this parent. Working with her questions—producing, improving, and prioritizing them—had given her a new understanding of why homework was assigned, why it was important for her to monitor her son's progress, and why homework is helpful to the teacher. She now saw herself as a partner with the teacher. The Question Formulation Technique changed the relationship between parent and teacher, yet it could easily fit within some of the traditional requests and invitations schools regularly extend to parents. Let's look more closely at the changes.

Changes for the Parent

- *Cognitive:* Ms. P talked about specific things she knows about asking questions that were new for her. She knew a way to help herself come up with questions. She knew the differences between closed- and open-ended questions. She knew how to change one type into another. She knew she could use questions to work on problems. She could more clearly describe what she understood about the problem.
- *Affective:* Ms. P smiled in the meeting, which is no small feat in a meeting focused on a problem with her son. She smiled because

she felt more comfortable talking about how to address the problem and was more confident that she could actually participate. She also smiled because the meeting wasn't about her worst fears: her son getting in trouble or being held back. Instead, she felt she could play a role in helping her child. This felt great.

- *Behavioral:* Ms. P had just done something she had never done before: she had produced several of her own questions, worked to improve them, and used specific criteria to prioritize them. She had done all of that rather than passively listen or try to respond to someone else's questions. She also made a specific plan for herself. She could now more effectively support her child's education, monitor his progress, advocate for him, and partner with the teacher.

Changes for the Teacher

- *Cognitive:* Ms. T had new ideas about the causes of S's problem and what to pay attention to. Her new understanding came from just listening to Ms. P's questions. Ms. T had new knowledge about what S's mother feared the most and what concerns needed to be assuaged before she could focus on how to help her son. She learned all of this by hearing Ms. P's questions.

- *Affective:* Ms. T had feelings she had rarely felt in meetings with parents about struggling students: relief, satisfaction, support, enlightenment, and even a little joy that she was not alone or working in opposition to S's mother but was rather in collaboration with her.

- *Behavioral:* Ms. T could now take concrete steps to help S. She would look even more closely at his homework to see what he was and was not understanding. She would also communicate regularly with her new partner, Ms. P, and demonstrate to S that she is working in collaboration with the most important adult in his life.

Changes for the Student

What has changed now for S? S knew he was accountable for turning in his homework. This was no small matter. Before, his mother was unaware of a problem—maybe even unaware that he had homework, much less that he was not doing it. He also knew that the most important adult in his life, his mother, and the most important adult at school, his teacher, were working together.

S was doing his homework and turning it in. He was reporting to his mother about what he had to do and was delivering the signed-off version to Ms. T. Doing the homework and getting some extra help, now that Ms. T could identify the challenge more readily, led to a cycle in which he actively sought out help when he didn't understand. His behavior settled down in class, and he participated more actively in class discussions. The partnership helped change his experience at school.

Changes for the School

What about the school? What did this new partnership mean for the entire school?

It conserved time and resources that could be used to address other challenges. S was not on a good trajectory; and if he performed poorly in classwork and began to act out, the school would need to respond in various ways. The assistant principal might have been asked to deal with behavioral or discipline problems. The school counselor might have been pulled in. The school may have started an IEP evaluation process that would require even more time and resources.

By taking the initiative to use the Question Formulation Technique with S's mother, Ms. T helped S have a better chance for success; invested in his mother's ability to support, monitor, and advocate for him throughout his school experience (not just in her classroom this year); and helped demonstrate to school leadership a different model for improving school-family partnerships.

A New Way to Build a Parent-School Partnership

Ms. T was a stellar example of a teacher as innovator and leader, taking the initiative as a problem solver and resource for students, parents, and school administrators. Now, thanks to her work, the school had one more parent able to play an effective role as a partner. Both Ms. T and Ms. P were now models for what could be done with all teachers and parents.

By using the Question Formulation Technique in one parent-teacher conference, Ms. T had created significant changes. A struggling student's parent became better able to partner with the teacher to address the problem. Ms. P learned to partner on this one issue, and she also developed universally relevant skills that can be repeatedly used.

Ms. T did not feel alone in facing the challenge. Moreover, she gained a replicable strategy for working with all parents, she mobilized a collaboration of important adults to support a struggling student, and the school gained another parent who can partner throughout her child's time at school. Though there is no guarantee that this will lead to better long-term educational outcomes for the child, the odds definitely went up in his favor.

Using the Question Formulation Technique with Individual Parents

As this case study illustrates, the Question Formulation Technique can be used with and by parents to think more deeply about and strategize more efficiently on how to address a range of issues in the course of a school year. Appendix B includes the following materials you can use with parents so they can produce and improve their own questions:

- Question Focus (QFocus) Design Template: the step-by-step process for creating a QFocus.
- Facilitating the Question Formulation Technique: a guide that includes the QFT steps, the facilitation process, and facilitation tips.
- Question Formulation Technique Worksheet: a handout (called "My List of Questions to Ask") designed for parents to come up with their own questions.
- QFT Sample Facilitation Timeframes: a rough guide meant to give you an idea about how much time to spend on each of the steps and how to adjust as needed.

This chapter has shared an example of using the Right Question Strategy in a teacher-initiated context. Chapter 3 will use a school-initiated change to show you how parents can support, monitor, and advocate to fully participate in their children's education.

Partnership Through School-Initiated Change

What Roles Can Parents Play in Their Children's Education?

Parents in low-income, minority, or immigrant communities do not necessarily see schools as welcoming institutions. Many parents, especially those who were not successful students themselves, may perceive an impassable moat separating them from the institution charged with educating their children. How can parents cross that moat? The school can let down the drawbridge and even warmly invite parents in, but parents still need to feel comfortable and clear about their role in order to enter into a partnership with the school.

The parents from whom we learned had never been considered sources of insight about improving education, nor had they been recognized as theorists about the idea and practice of parent involvement. But we see it differently. The parents with whom we have worked not only named a long overlooked problem that needed to be addressed but also helped organically construct a theory of effective action. It is indeed a theory because it represents a coherent group of tested general propositions that can be used as principles of explanation and prediction. Look at the relevance of their principles of effective action from kindergarten through high school. Here are the three roles they need to be able to play in order to partner effectively with their children's educators:

- *Support* their children's education.
- *Monitor* their academic, social, and emotional progress.
- *Advocate* for their children when necessary.

Each role contributes to a student's success. When all three are combined, however, parents can be truly effective partners with the school. The interaction among the three roles is complex. Notice in the following descriptions how each role connects to the other two.

Support

Parents regularly receive information about how to *support* their children's education. This can range from household matters such as making sure children have regular bedtimes and eat breakfast to schoolwork matters of setting aside a space and time to do homework.

There's nothing wrong with these recommendations, but they need to be accompanied by the next step up the ladder of effective parent engagement: *monitoring*. If a child has space to do homework and is well fed, and a general message about the importance of education permeates the home, what more should parents do?

Monitor

Parents must regularly take the pulse of what's happening for their children at school. They need to have a sense of the workload, make sure the work is being done, review report cards and other materials coming home, and, in general, keep an eye on their children's learning and social and emotional needs. The act of monitoring—of keeping an eye on current status and progress—builds upon the step of supporting a child's education. Supporting and monitoring should go hand-in-hand. They complement each other. They are necessary for effective parent participation, but they are not sufficient for an effective partnership.

Advocate

What happens when a parent, monitoring a child's school experience and progress, notices a problem, sees a reluctance to go to school, observes that the child is not doing well, and even gets a report card confirming that? What is the parent to do? Clearly, if there's a problem—noticed because the parent is indeed actively monitoring—some kind of action is necessary. In the same way that a teacher might work with the child first, before contacting the parent (as Ms. T did in the previous chapter), the parent may need to reach out to the teacher or the school to proactively address emerging problems.

Each role has its own unique value, but playing just one role, while effective, may limit the parent-school partnership's power. Indeed, even a parent confident enough to advocate for a child will be at a great disadvantage in collaborating with the school if the advocacy is not informed by the information gathered through actively supporting and monitoring the child's progress. By contrast, a parent who is supporting a child's education, monitoring progress, and ready and able to advocate when necessary has climbed the partnership ladder (see Figure 3.1). At the top of that ladder, the parent—full of passion for the child, clear about his or her role, and equipped with the powerful skill of question formulation—can be an effective and strategic partner in working to ensure that student's success.

The parent is an invaluable resource for the teacher and the schools. Teachers, from primary to high school, can have anywhere

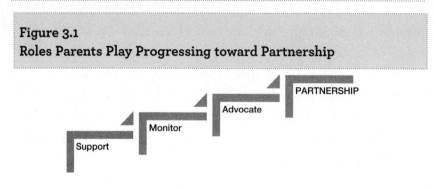

Figure 3.1
Roles Parents Play Progressing toward Partnership

from 20 to 160 students pass through their classrooms each day. How can any teacher stay on top of every student every day who might be stumbling, or just hesitating, or in some way falling behind?

Helping All Parents Learn to Play All Three Roles

There's a lot already on the plate of administrators and teachers. There are plenty of good reasons and competing, more urgent demands that result in relegating "work with parents" to perhaps one staff person in the building or to an occasional activity. Given how little time and how few resources are available, it is crucial to find a way to make it easier for schools to work with parents productively. This case study demonstrates how, during a common school event—an open house—parents can learn about three distinct roles they can play, acquire the specific skill of question formulation to help them play those roles, and begin to collaborate with the school in addressing a schoolwide problem that affects all children.

For this open house, the school has decided to eschew its traditional efforts of simply transmitting information and instead will jumpstart a collaborative problem-solving process by engaging parents in thinking about how the whole community can better address the school's growing bullying problem. The school has become increasingly aware of the influence of social and emotional factors on learning. Indeed, the field of social and emotional learning (SEL) directly lays out the connection between social and emotional risk factors and their impact on academic outcomes (Durlak, Weissberg, Dymnicki, Taylor, & Schellinger, 2011; Smith & Low, 2013). The open house is the initial step of a longer process that will continue throughout the year.

Case Study: A New Kind of Open House

Planning to Use the Question Formulation Technique

A quick initial conversation between Ms. AP, the new assistant principal, and Ms. C, the school counselor, about bullying behavior observed just two weeks into the school year was the catalyst for using the QFT with parents at the open house. When Ms. AP met with Mr. P, the principal, he voiced concerns about how one or two of the most vocal and most negative parents might hog the floor. Ms. C referred to the teachers she'd observed skillfully facilitating the QFT and made the case for passing the task to them, which would get parents thinking collaboratively about solutions to the problem and showcase a process used with their children in class.

The principal gave Ms. C the green light—a little nervously—and she recruited teacher volunteers to use the QFT at an upcoming open house that night. The teachers were excited, for they realized that this was a new way of using some of the open house time. The open house could provide an opportunity to start a dialogue with the parent community about how best to partner to create a safe, caring environment for all students. Over the next few weeks, school staff, who wanted as many parents as possible to attend, consulted with the parent liaison and then sought the help of current parent leaders to assist in reaching out and recruiting parents to come to the open house. As they got closer to the night of the open house, they planned how best to use the QFT. Ms. AP suggested they introduce parents not only to the Question Formulation Technique but also to the Support, Monitor, and Advocate model for roles they can play.

Designing the Question Focus

The group quickly got to work on designing the Question Focus (QFocus). It was essential, they felt, to give *all* parents (not just "the problem student's" parents or the "victim's" parents) an opportunity to ask questions and share different perspectives. It would help expand everyone's thinking about the issue—administrators, teachers, and parents—and lead to a better plan for moving forward. They came up with some variations on the theme for the QFocus:

- Respectful Behavior
- Our Responsibilities to One Another
- A Caring Environment
- Creating a Caring Environment

They realized that the first one, "Respectful Behavior," would put too much attention on the word *behavior,* a live wire they did not want to start with because most parents' first fear is that their child is *not* behaving well. The second one, "Our Responsibilities to One Another," might too quickly get people thinking about who is *not* being responsible and provoke defensiveness about being perceived as the source of the problem. "A Caring Environment" offered some room for positive definitional work and thinking, but it might be a little too abstract. "Creating a Caring Environment" felt different. The notion of "creating" opened up thinking about an action, and there was an implicit sense of mutual responsibility for making it happen.

They talked briefly about the importance of creating that space for mutual responsibility. Ms. AP got excited, saying, "It's really about mutual accountability. We all need to be accountable for creating a caring environment—administrators, teachers, parents, *and* students. Students get the difference between 'talking the talk' and 'walking the walk.' Plus, using this QFocus will help us actually define *caring environment* as well. It also fits perfectly with wanting to talk about the roles parents can play."

That was it. They had their QFocus: "Creating a Caring Environment." There was a mixed, but palpable, sense of relief and excitement. The hard design work had been done. The teachers have learned through their own experiences that designing a Question Focus gets easier the more you do it. But, in this case, they were pretty proud of themselves for they were able to take that QFocus design skill and apply it in a whole new way, to an entirely different situation from their classroom teaching and learning purposes.

Ms. F, the 4th grade teacher, said, "We'll need to clarify the prioritization instructions for when we ask parents to choose their three top questions. Do we want to have them look at their questions with an eye to understanding and defining the problem or challenge, or with thoughts about what can be done?"

Ms. AP, realizing that there's more to the QFT than had met her eye during her classroom observations, said, "I don't really understand. Don't you just ask them to come up with the three questions they consider most important?"

"Well," Ms. F responded, "that is a basic version, and it's fine. We've also learned that you can get more specific with prioritization instructions based on where the students are going and what they'll be doing with their questions. I think the same applies here. What would really be the most important things for parents to be thinking about when they are choosing their priority questions?"

Ms. C, the counselor, experienced in thinking about the strengths that different parties can bring to a problem, commented, "If they've asked a lot of questions about creating a caring environment, could we ask them to choose three questions about the roles parents can play in helping create that environment?"

Ms. F countered, "I think that might be too narrow. Plus, it puts all of the emphasis on the parents, and we talked about how we are all mutually accountable to one another." Ms. C concurred. Ms. F, experienced in using the QFT, thought about Ms. AP's comment about mutual accountability, and her face lit up with a new idea.

"They are going to want answers from us," she said. "They won't leave satisfied if we have them generate questions and then we don't answer them—at least those we can answer on the spot. Here's something I do with my students when they're starting a research project. It may be relevant here. Let's ask the parents to choose three questions they'll want to get an answer to right away. This helps my students see that sometimes you have to sequence questions, and some questions can only be answered after you have obtained some initial information. It helps sharpen their use of questions." Her suggestion was strongly seconded by another teacher, and the group decided to go with it.

Open House Night

Parents filed into the gym where the open house is traditionally held and noticed, immediately, that something was different. Instead of rows of seats, the gym was full of rectangular tables with eight chairs placed around each one. This clearly was not the setup for spending 45 minutes listening to speakers.

At 6:30 p.m., Mr. P, the principal, got things started by welcoming them all and sharing some words about the high expectations and aspirations the school has for their children and a special commitment the school is making to ensure that as students study the content in all subject areas, they are also learning "what's called '21st century skills' for thinking, problem solving, and cooperating that will help them in school and beyond in life and work." Ms. AP also welcomed the families and then shared that she, a team of teachers, and the school counselor had worked hard on the plan for the evening and were excited that it would give them a chance to hear and learn more from parents. She introduced the planning team members and explained that everyone was going to be asked to participate in some group work during the meeting. "But, before we do that," she continued, "I just wanted to share with you some of our thoughts about the important roles you can play in your children's education."

On the screen behind her, the word *SUPPORT* appeared and beneath it a simple definition. "In this role, you help, encourage, and provide for your children. You might also support the work of teachers and the school on your children's behalf. We will not be sharing your thoughts, but think about one thing you do to support your children." She gave parents a few seconds to think before offering some examples.

"For example, you provide for your children's basic needs, provide a space for studying, make sure they get enough sleep, and so forth. In fact, this is the primary role many schools encourage parents to play. Certainly, students benefit from this kind of support at home, but we have also learned about how helpful it is to your children and to our students when you play another role."

The screen behind her displayed the word *MONITOR* and beneath it a simple definition. "In this role, you keep track of your children's progress and pay attention to their needs. You can monitor children's entire school experience, how they are doing academically and socially, and how the school is meeting their needs. Please think now about one thing you do to monitor your children's education." She paused again so parents could think about how they were monitoring—for example, by monitoring what their children are learning, noticing any challenges they are encountering, and checking their homework.

"If you are supporting your children's education in different ways, and you are paying attention to how they are doing, maybe signing off on homework if the teacher has requested that, and you are keeping an eye on their work and on how they feel about school, then you are greatly helping your child already. This might be all that schools encourage you to do, but we see the value of you playing another role."

Finally, the word *ADVOCATE* appeared on the screen but without a definition. "In this role," Ms. AP explained, "based on what you are monitoring and observing about your children, there will be times when you need to reach out to us. You'll speak up, draw our attention to some problems we might be missing, and you may even make specific requests on behalf of your children. Lastly, please think of one situation in which you have advocated for your children. Think about the specific situation and what exactly you did."

Ms. AP paused and again gave a few seconds for parents to think before sharing different ways they could advocate. "You can also be advocates for meeting the needs of all children and address issues individually or as part of an organized group at the classroom, school, or district level.

"We are trying, every day, to meet the needs of all—and we mean *all*—students in this school. But," she added, laughing a little, "there are more of them than there are of us. Have you ever felt outnumbered by your kids? Imagine 1,200 of them! You love 'em all, but they're a handful. That's why we know we benefit not only when you are supporting your child at home but also when you are keeping track of their work and progress. We know that every child can benefit from an advocate, from someone in her or his corner. Sometimes, they may not like you there, but you know and we know how important that is.

"Encouraging you to play all three roles might go beyond what most schools actively promote, but we know that all students will do better when they have the most important adults in their lives, at home and school, working together. Supporting your child's education at home, monitoring their progress, and advocating for them when necessary can help make that partnership possible. Now, take a minute and think about one more thing you would like to do to support, monitor, and advocate."

Ms. AP then showed on the screen the three words shaped in the form of a ladder, modeled on Arnstein's (1969) Ladder of Citizen Participation, which details the difference between being involved and being a full partner:

PARTNERSHIP

ADVOCATE

MONITOR

SUPPORT

"Playing these three roles can lead to a partnership with us. For our part, we want to make sure that you can easily play those three roles. But partnership is a two-way street. So we commit to informing you—to keep you in the loop on what is happening for your children and here at the school; inviting your participation; and collaborating, including ways that we are going to work together tonight to address a problem.

"So, as part of that commitment to hear from you, we've designed this open house a little differently. We have introduced you to the three roles you can play. In a moment, we are going to use a process that many of your children have used in the classroom, and the same process is being used in many other places as well, including colleges, medical schools, and even community organizations and large corporations. It is a process that will allow us to hear your questions." She then presented a slide with references to *Make Just One Change: Teach Students to Ask Their Own Questions* (Rothstein & Santana, 2011); presentations to Microsoft, Harvard Medical School, and other well-known institutions; and articles in the medical literature referring to rigorous research funded by the National Institutes of Health on the Right Question Strategy. When preparing the PowerPoint, she felt it was important to demonstrate to parents that the school respected them by offering the opportunity to spend time on a process that had been used not only by their children but also by some of the most respected institutions in the country. She and her colleagues felt that using the QFT with parents was a sign of deep respect for what their questions can add to the school.

"We have a team of teachers who are helping us tonight. One of them will be joining you at your table as a recorder. Ms. F, a 4th grade teacher, is going to lead us all through the Question Formulation Technique to look at an issue that is important for helping us help your students succeed. She's a real expert in leading this so we're in good hands. We'll spend about 25 minutes on this before you head off to hear from teachers in their classrooms."

Starting the Question Formulation Technique

Ms. F asked the teachers to join the groups, chart paper and markers in hand, and she invited everyone at the table to introduce themselves by sharing their names and the name and grade of their child/children at the school. Then she started facilitating the process.

"We're going to use the Question Formulation Technique to come up with some questions about a topic I'll present to you in a moment. Then you'll do some more work with your questions and prioritize them, and then we'll hear in the large group some ideas on what we've learned by working together in this process." She ended by presenting a slide of the four rules.

The Rules for Producing Questions

1. Ask as many questions as you can.
2. Do not stop to discuss, judge, or answer the questions.
3. Write down every question in the exact way it is stated.
4. Change any statements into questions.

She then asked parents to talk at their tables about what they might find difficult about following the rules, and after a minute of conversation at the table, she asked for people to share. One parent near the front of the room said, "When a question is asked, you are kind of expecting to talk about it right away." Ms. F, realizing that the whole room could not hear her, repeated the comment and then asked for other thoughts. Another parent, this time from the back of the room and loud enough for all to hear, said, "Sometimes it's just hard to come up with more than one question, so the first rule might be hard." Then another chimed in: "It can be hard to not judge something right away. The same goes with hearing questions that maybe don't make any sense."

Ms. F thanked them and briefly talked about how the QFT process can feel a little uncomfortable at first. "So don't feel bad if it's a little awkward," she said. "Each teacher writing the questions down will be waiting for questions to come. Remember, be sure your teacher writes down the questions exactly as you asked them! OK, let's get started," she said enthusiastically. "Now the only thing you'll be doing is asking questions for the next three minutes without any discussion. Here's the topic—the focus for *your* questions: many of you have heard in the news that bullying is a problem in some schools. We want you to help us think about this problem differently."

She presented the slide with the Question Focus: "Creating a Caring Environment."

It was greeted with what the principal would later describe as a "nerve-wracking, deafening silence." The parents had never before been invited to jump into a thinking activity at the school like this. Ms. F waited for about 10 seconds and then said, "Just ask anything that comes to mind. Don't hold back. There is no wrong question here."

That little addition—"no wrong question"—produced a quick change in body language. It was as if the parents were relieved to know that they weren't going to be getting this assignment wrong.

They were, after all, at school, and many of them did not feel confident that they knew enough to talk about their children's education and that helped maintain a silence, even though they had been invited to share. It's one of the unstated but strongly perceived differences in power, knowledge, and expertise that parents feel when engaging with the school. School staff might have the best of intentions, but if parents feel uncomfortable participating and voicing their opinions, then the silence will indeed be "deafening." Once parents heard they would not be judged "wrong" for any question they asked, the noise picked up in the room as the questions started coming.

Producing Questions About Creating a Caring Environment

Ms. C was the scribe at one of the tables as a couple of parents started to ask questions, including "What do they mean by *caring*?" Ms. F, standing near that group, understood immediately, just from that one question, how parents might again be deferring to the school staff, expecting that they know what this is all about. She heard a similar question reflecting a similar expectation that the school will tell parents what they should be thinking and asking questions about.

Understanding that this really was a different kind of process than most parents have experienced, certainly at the school, she spoke up to the whole group, having to wait until one already active table quieted down. "Remember: there is no wrong question here, and it's not as if we know the right questions to ask. We really just want to hear your questions, whatever questions you have about this statement," and she pointed again to the Question Focus on the screen: Creating a Caring Environment.

A couple of the teachers now seemed to relax a bit for they had been encountering a similar response at their tables and didn't know quite how to handle it. This last encouraging statement from Ms. F got things moving more smoothly. Ms. C's group moved on from the first question:

1. What do they mean by *caring*?
2. Is there a problem?
3. Is this about a caring environment in the school?
4. What about after school?
5. Is this because of the fight that happened last year?

Then a sixth question: (6) "What fight?" The parent who asked that question really wanted an immediate answer. A couple of parents started to respond. Ms. C didn't know if she should cut them off to stay on the questioning task, when another parent said, "I think we're supposed to be just asking questions. We can answer them later." Ms. C was relieved, but the parent who wanted to know right now about the particulars of the fight seemed a little frustrated. One of the parents told her, "I'll tell you about it later." The rest of the group was ready to move ahead, and Ms. C repeated the QFocus again, "Creating a caring environment." The list grew.

7. Who's creating it?
8. What does *a caring environment* mean?
9. Does it mean just keep the kids from fighting?

At this point, Ms. C was doing her best to restrain herself from violating the second rule by judging a question. She had to keep herself from showing her approval or disapproval of any question because, again, the power disparity between school staff and parents would only communicate that one parent's question is judged as better than another's. She already knew that question 7—"Who's creating it?"—would provide an opportunity for school staff *and* parents to have a conversation about the "who." And question 8 was exactly the kind of definitional question that would help them work together to answer that question—to really define what a caring environment looks like.

Ms. AP gave the groups a time warning, saying that they'd need to wrap up their last questions. When Ms. C's group finished, they had come up with 13 questions in 5 minutes:

1. What do they mean by *caring*?
2. Is there a problem?
3. Is this about a caring environment in the school?
4. What about after school?
5. Is this because of the fight that happened last year?
6. What fight?
7. Who's creating it?
8. What does *a caring environment* mean?
9. Does it mean just keep the kids from fighting?
10. Do the kids know what's expected of them?
11. Are parents part of this?
12. Is there something we can do to help?
13. What should the school be doing?

Open- and Closed-Ended Questions

Ms. F then displayed a slide with the following terms and their definitions:

- *Closed-ended questions* can be answered with a simple *yes, no,* or a one-word answer.
- *Open-ended questions* require more explanation.

In her group, Ms. C said, "I'd like you to look at the list of questions you came up with and mark the closed-ended ones with a *C* and the open ones with an *O*." She positioned the list of questions so people could gather around and look at them together.

The group seemed stuck by the first question, "What do they mean by *caring*?" One parent said, "Well, there's got to be an answer to that, so isn't that closed?" Another parent said, "Maybe, but it's not one word, or there might be a difference of opinion." The group nodded in agreement, as did the first parent, and they labeled the first question with an *O*. They moved through the rest of the list, talked a bit about question 4 ("What about after school?"), and thought it might fall into both categories.

Once done with categorizing, Ms. F led the group through a discussion of advantages and disadvantages of asking closed- and open-ended questions. "Let's think for a minute about the two types of questions you have on your list. What will be some advantages and disadvantages of asking the closed-ended questions? I would like to get a couple of examples." She then gathered a few advantages, including the ability to get quick, clear, and specific answers. Disadvantages include the fact that answers don't provide much information and may close the conversation. She continued, "Now, what will be some advantages and disadvantages of asking open-ended questions?" Again, she gathered a few responses: advantages are that you get more information and they open up the conversation to further discussion, and disadvantages are that they're time consuming and too much information can potentially be confusing. Ms. F concluded, "As you can see, there are advantages and disadvantages to asking both types of questions. Each one has value, depending on the kind of information you want to get."

Then they tackled the next task: changing the questions.

"Now," said Ms. F, "take a closed-ended question and turn it into an open-ended one and then do the opposite—take an open and close it down."

One parent looked at question 2 and said, "We can change that from 'Is there a problem?' to 'What is the problem?'" The parents looked for an open-ended one to close down and focused on question 8, changing it from "What does *a caring environment* mean?" to "Does the school know what it means?"

Ms. C was struck by how they really were thinking that the school has an answer to this. One parent got jazzed about changing more of the questions, saying, "It really makes you think different to ask it another way." She wanted them to work on one last question: "Are parents part of this?"

Prioritization

Before they could get to work on it, Ms. F was saying to the whole room, "We're ready to move on to the prioritization step and choose some important questions." She deliberately did not say *the* most important because she knew that would only reinforce the suspicion that the school knows what the three most important questions are and the parents should try to figure that out.

"Review your list of questions and choose three questions that you'll want to get an answer to right away." Her criteria for prioritization here were subtle. The instruction to choose questions "you'll want to get an answer to right away" would result in the parents setting a learning agenda that they owned. That sense of ownership, she knew from her experience in the classroom, made all the difference between someone waiting to be informed or directed versus someone who is actively engaged in thinking and getting answers.

"You have five minutes to select those three questions," Ms. F announced, leaving a slide up of the criteria and instructions. The groups got to work. In Ms. C's group, they looked again at their original list of 13 questions and the ones they changed, which added more questions:

1. What do they mean by *caring*?
2. Is there a problem?
3. Is this about a caring environment inside the school?
4. What about after school?
5. Is this because of the fight that happened last year?
6. What fight?
7. Who's creating it?
8. What does *a caring environment* mean?

9. Does it mean just keep the kids from fighting?
10. Do the kids know what's expected of them?
11. Are parents part of this?
12. Is there something we can do to help?
13. What should the school be doing?
14. What is the problem? (changed from 2)
15. Does the school know what it means? (changed from 8)

By now, the group was not hesitating or looking to Ms. C for approval. They jumped right in. Interestingly, the parent who wanted to know about the fight was now eager to prioritize other questions.

"Look at question 13, 'What should the school be doing?' We need to know about the work of the school in dealing with this issue. This question will help us understand what the school needs to do, if they are doing it, and what could be improved."

Another parent piped up as if she had just realized something. "Remember those three roles we should be playing? We need to ask about that."

"Is there something we can do to help?" one suggested.

A couple of parents, with their new awareness of open- and closed-ended questions, spoke at the same time and said, "What can we do to help?"

The group broke into laughter about how they pounced on that new version of their question.

Ms. F has been circulating around the room as the groups were working and was pleased to see that there was both common ground to questioning among all of the groups as well as some different emphases from group to group. For example, she noticed another group's list of questions went right to clarifying the statement's meaning, specific words' meanings, and implications about what is and is not happening at the school. Near the end, she noted, they also got to questions about their roles.

Questions from Different Groups

In Ms. F's perusal of the work done by more groups, she saw how the kinds of questions the parents were asking added to her own understanding of what the school, the community, and students need to be thinking about. All of these questions actually offered a shortcut to getting people to think deeply about the meaning of a caring environment and what's required in order to create one.

Group 2

1. What is *a caring environment*?
2. What is in the environment?
3. What does it mean to create it?
4. Why does it need to be created?
5. What is going on?
6. Doesn't the school have it now?
7. Is this a need the school has?
8. Is this something new?
9. What do the students think about this?
10. Is this being done to correct something?
11. What will be needed in order to create it?
12. Is there something I'm expected to do?
13. Who will be involved?
14. How will it be different from how the school works now?

Group 3

1. Why?
2. Is there a problem?
3. Whose idea is this?
4. What will make the environment caring?
5. Is this in response to a problem?
6. What has been done to improve the environment?
7. Who will be creating this environment?
8. What experience do they have doing this?

9. What will be the options?

10. What is the goal?

11. What would it take?

12. Is the current environment not caring?

13. What do you mean by *caring*?

Group 4

1. Why do you need to create a caring environment?

2. Was the environment ever caring?

3. Is this a new trend?

4. Are you trying to address a problem with this proposal?

5. What is *caring*?

6. Who will be deciding on the kind of caring environment?

7. What does it mean to have *a caring environment*?

8. How can we be part of this?

9. Will staff need training?

10. How will children be learning about this caring environment?

The process produced a lot of energized discussion in the room. "This," Mr. P, the principal, thought, "is certainly a very different kind of open house. I didn't quite know if they'd be able to pull it off. They did—and more."

Next Steps

The session was not done yet. Ms. F would have liked to have spent some more time on next steps, but she simply had to summarize that all of the questions would be typed up and shared on the website. "They will help us start our work with you, the staff, and students this year on how to create actions steps for all of us to take in building the best caring environment possible. There are some questions that we'll be able to answer immediately, and we plan to share those answers with you by next week. There are other questions that I can see will open up our thinking and will help us include your perspectives and priorities as we work on this together."

Reflection

Ms. F did not want the parents to miss out on the important reflection step in the Question Formulation Technique. She wanted them to have a chance to think about what they learned by working with their questions. She told the whole crowd, "Please take two minutes to quickly share what you've learned at your tables, and then we'll hear some examples from the whole group."

Her reflection question was very simple: "What did you learn?"

One parent said, "I like this way of thinking with other parents. I got to hear questions I never would have thought of on my own." Another parent added, "I never thought much before about how the way you ask a question can make a difference in the information you get. I can really use this, especially when I go to the doctor. I never know if I'm asking the right questions there when I take my kids. Now I can prepare some questions ahead of time."

Just then, Ms. F added one more reflection question: "What did you learn from thinking about support, monitor, and advocate roles?"

In Ms. C's group, one parent talked about her new awareness about the roles and how she was mostly playing one role, supporting, was less often monitoring, and was rarely advocating. Another parent said, "Yeah, it is very important to know about the roles we can play and how each role is needed. That shows me we just don't think enough about that. Just like Ms. AP said at the beginning, our kids need us to do that!"

Ms. AP stood up again in front of the whole room and thanked all of the participants. "These questions are going to help us this year as we all work on creating a warm, caring environment for our students. We know that students need to feel safe, cared for, and supported in order to even begin to do their academic work. We are committing to ensure that happens throughout the school. Make sure to actively support, monitor, and advocate as needed! Before you head off to your classrooms, let's give the teachers who worked at your tables a chance to get there, and let's give them, Ms. F, and *you* a round of applause for the great work you all did." As they walked out, they each received a cardstock sheet of paper with the definitions of *support, monitor,* and *advocate* along with all the steps of the Question Formulation Technique.

Building a Partnership

As we just saw, the open house can serve as an opportunity to strengthen parents' capacity to partner effectively with the school and collaborate in problem solving. Karen Mapp (2003), of the Harvard Graduate School of Education, has long argued that schools need to make changes in order to better use events such as an open house. We entirely agree and also think, that given the many demands on school staff, that we need to find the simplest, most efficient, and most productive ways to make such changes.

Any school that wants to invest in parents' capacity to partner more effectively can follow the example presented in this chapter (see also Appendix B for tools on how to implement what you read about in this chapter in your own school). Parents can walk away with a stronger skill of question formulation as well as a succinct and useful "theory of effective participation" to guide their actions. The school can tap more partners to help address a schoolwide problem such as bullying.

The open house started the process of collaboration in a substantive, meaningful way. It did not solve the problem or end the problem-solving process. Instead, the integration of aspects of the Right Question Strategy into an already existing format for parent-school interaction made for a very productive evening. The idea of spending time on questions may seem to some people like a digression or even a detour when there's so much information that could be shared with parents. What seems like a detour turns, however, into a shortcut to a more effective partnership and better outcomes for students. The open house in this case study was an example of a school working on events it had already scheduled and finding a way to turn that task into an important learning and community-building experience. Just consider the significance of the changes for parents and school stakeholders.

Changes for Parents

- *Cognitive:* Parents left the open house with new knowledge about a process for producing, improving, and prioritizing their questions. They talked about how they "knew how to ask questions" better than ever before. They also left with a simple and useful framework to organize their thinking about the roles they can play in their children's education. They could describe what they now knew about the differences and complementary aspects of supporting their children's education, monitoring their progress, and advocating for them when necessary. "I never quite thought about it that way, but it makes so much sense. My kids need me to be there for them and now I understand better what role I can play."
- *Affective:* The changes in parents were palpable. They were smiling and laughing with one another; instead of the stony silence evident in numerous events, they were animated and talkative as they filed out of the room. Many shared how they now felt more confident about playing a role in their children's education. They felt respected by the school and appreciative of the opportunity to learn a strategy that could have great value for them in their own lives and as participants in their children's education. They also walked away with a new sense of purpose and a feeling of urgency that they needed to be actively in communication with the school. Moreover, there was a new and very strong sense of community. One parent said, "I've just

never talked to as many parents about our kids' education as I did tonight. I used to feel like I was the only one who didn't know quite what to do to help. When I heard some of the other questions and the conversation, I realized I'm not alone, and now there are more parents I can talk to."

- *Behavioral:* The changes were evident immediately during the QFT process and, it turns out, continued long after the open house. These are no small changes. Parents were now able to formulate their own questions to use strategically in their new partnership with the school.

In the months following the open house, school staff saw new levels of involvement as parents responded to communications from the school. Even more, parents from whom they had never heard before were now initiating communication with the school. Parents attended follow-up meetings, discussed answers to the questions raised that night, and began to collaborate with school staff in prioritizing next steps. School staff also began to see the parents as a resource and as strong allies for creating a more caring environment. They opened up to new ways for the parents to become involved, including as volunteers and an "extra set of eyes" in settings where some of the problems had been popping up.

Perhaps most significant, parents were actively playing the three roles more consistently. Parents were quicker to respond to messages from teachers, homework was monitored and submitted, and more parents prepared questions to ask at parent-teacher conferences. One teacher noted, "We've never had these kinds of productive conversations that we now have with parents who are using the QFT on their own." The principal was getting a few more phone calls, but now they were coming from parents who were prepared with specific questions and who wanted to work in partnership with the school.

By the end of the year, everyone—school leadership, faculty, parents, and students—was contributing to creating a caring environment.

Discipline problems dropped significantly, and the teachers and students now had more time and energy to focus on academic progress.

Changes for the School

This simple shift in the way the time of the open house was used produced striking changes for the school. The event launched a process for collaborative problem solving with parents. The parents' questions not only provided a window into what they were most concerned about but also helped stimulate new lines of thought for school staff as they all explored how to improve school climate and create a caring environment.

The success of the event also gave the school a new model for hosting open houses, encouraging parent participation, and creating a more effective partnership with parents. There was also a new sense of community. Parents worked with school staff, especially teachers, in a radically different way from anything they had done before.

Many other school events and activities, not only open houses, can be redesigned and used as opportunities to invest in parents and build strong partnerships and to address any issue, not just bullying as this chapter's case study explored. Family nights, Title I monthly meetings, and parent workshops are other contexts in which parents can learn about their three specific roles and sharpen their question-asking skills. Figure 3.2 shares some ideas for using the Right Question Strategy with groups of parents at such events.

Changes for Students

Students benefited from parents who were playing an active role on an ongoing basis. Thanks to the work the school initiated, the parents now were clear about their different roles. When parents are aware of their roles, they are more likely to participate in their

Figure 3.2

Using the Right Question Strategy with Groups of Parents

Handout (see Appendix B)	Tips for Use
1. Integrating the Right Question Strategy into School Activities	Use this template to plan how to incorporate the strategy into a school event.
2. Three Roles Parents Can Play: Support, Monitor, and Advocate	This short guide includes definitions of the three key roles parents can play and suggestions for facilitating an activity to introduce them.
3. Facilitating the Question Formulation Technique (QFT) with Groups of Parents	This guide describes the QFT process and includes suggestions for effective facilitation in a group setting. It includes two sample facilitation time frames.
4. Support, Monitor, and Advocate: A Model for Effective Parent Participation in Their Children's Education	This handout offers definitions of the three roles parents can play. You can use it as a handout as you introduce the roles or for parents to review after the session.
5. Supporting, Monitoring, and Advocating Action Plan	Use this template to facilitate a full activity in which parents name how they play each of the three roles. You may also distribute the template to parents at the end of the session to review and think further about the roles.
6. Question Formulation Technique (QFT) Template	Distribute this handout at the end of the session for parents to review all of the steps in the QFT process.

children's education in comparison to parents who are unaware of the roles they can play (Hoover-Dempsey & Sandler, 1997). The thinking skill of question formulation gives parents new confidence to play those roles. Their children now have strong partners behind them, working together.

As the principal noted, he is always going to hear from a few parents who will want to take up more time than he has to give them. For him, it's clear that "we need to invest in all parents. If we have more parents supporting, monitoring, and advocating, then we're going to have a stronger community, a more successful school, and students who will benefit from both."

When we were developing these ideas based on what we were learning from the parents, we caught a glimpse of the potential of the support, monitor, and advocate roles as an explanatory resource. It could help parents organize their thinking about what kinds of action to take once they had the skill of question formulation. We did not, however, fully understand then that the parents had demonstrated a theory of effective participation.

Its theoretical strength was validated by experts on many levels who offered it the sincerest form of flattery: imitation. The three terms—*support, monitor,* and *advocate*—were adopted widely, sometimes with a full understanding of their value and sometimes as just another set of words to slip into a buffet of parent involvement options. We observed that foundations supporting parent involvement, such as the DeWitt Wallace-Reader's Digest Funds and the Kellogg Foundation (2013), included these three terms in their criteria for funding. Parent leadership programs, such as the Commonwealth Institute for Parent Leadership program of the Prichard Committee (2012), produced tote bags that featured the phrase *Support, Monitor, and Advocate.* Eventually, even the U.S. Department of Education in 2009 embedded the words in their guidelines for effective parent participation.

The theory, as first demonstrated by the parents with whom we worked two decades ago, is worthy of respect and emulation. However, these three roles—support, monitor, and advocate—are not just a few of the many things that could be suggested for parents. They are the foundation for building a strong partnership between schools and families.

An IEP Partnership Through Parent Liaison–Initiated Change

In districts around the country, schools struggle to provide appropriate special education services to students who need them. Costs keep skyrocketing; the range of needs that could require special education keep expanding; and the pressure on schools mount, day by day, as students' scores on high-stakes tests are used to assess a school's effectiveness.

Another concern is also at play in special education: many schools and districts have begun to look closely at data showing a disproportionately high number of referrals to special education for rambunctious young boys and especially boys of color. The data indicate that gender and racial biases may be in play (Alexander, 2010; Andrews, Wisniewski, & Mulick, 1997; Blanchett, 2006).

Parents also are struggling with assessing their children's special education needs. They are often shocked, upset, or confused when they hear that the school wants to refer their child for testing to determine need and eligibility for special education services and an Individualized Education Plan (IEP). They have been on the outside, without access to daily classroom observation. Aside, perhaps, from "concerns about behavior" that show up in an occasional report card, they may not even be aware of the struggles their children are having or how best to address them.

The decision to refer a child to special education testing is no small matter. Immediately, the school has to marshal significant resources to conduct the assessment. Then, if deemed necessary, the time, personnel, and funding required for carrying out a full IEP consumes even greater resources.

The Problem

The IEP process is the most explicit practice that exists for a school-family partnership. After all, it is based on a law that requires not only school-family collaboration but also the parent's signed consent. What could be better? The sad truth is that almost anything could be better than the current reality; many school-parent partnerships around the IEP are far from ideal. Schools may be on the defensive if there is a concern (e.g., yet another referral reflecting bias). They are also under extraordinary budgetary pressures that make it difficult to commit to a wide range of services needed for implementing the IEP, not to mention intense test score pressures, as they try to accommodate special testing arrangements for students with an IEP while improving the entire school's test results.

For parents, a request to refer a child for special education testing can set off a roller coaster of emotions. This first step in some ways suggests the parents' power in this context. The parent is being asked to give permission for their child to be tested. It will not proceed unless the parent says "yes." The parent has veto power.

Parents, however, rarely feel powerful. The request for a child to be tested is typically a painful trigger for parental anxiety, insecurities, and fears that "there is something wrong with my child." Then the parents face another challenge: the imbalance in knowledge and experience contributes to their feelings of inadequacy when trying to participate in the IEP meeting. School staff have savvy, insider knowledge about the whole process and system, and parents are the outsiders being invited in to participate in a vast array of decisions, from prereferrals, identification of the particular issue or disability, determination of eligibility, development of the IEP, determination of goals, and accommodations and services—not to mention the implementation of the IEP, assessment of its effectiveness, possible adjustments, and the periodic reviews to assess progress and action steps (Katz, 2015; Kupper, 2000). It is a long, demanding, complicated, and emotional journey.

For many parents who are unaccustomed to advocating for their children, inexperienced in partnering with educators in any situation, and not fluent in English or familiar with educational jargon, the process can be painful and frustrating. Parents have often told us, "I didn't understand what was being said, so I just sat there and nodded most of the time. I was embarrassed to say I didn't understand, and I was just sad thinking about my child." However, there are also parents who express deep appreciation for the school if they feel supported and welcomed. They are comfortable entrusting the decision making to school staff: "I know that they wanted to help my son, and that made me feel really good. I just trust that they know what they are doing, and I am happy to give my permission."

In either case, not understanding or fully trusting a professional's decision-making wisdom means the parent is hardly a partner in the process. This is no secret. Many states now have passionate advocacy organizations often started by parents who themselves were once bewildered and overwhelmed by the complexity of the IEP process.

They offer comprehensive guides and advocacy suggestions for parents, with translations not only into the native languages of many ELL parents but also of unfamiliar jargon into plain English. Advocacy organizations and even legal representation can be an invaluable resource for some parents, but these supports are not readily available in most low-income communities.

Building Foundational Skills to Participate Effectively in the IEP Process

The Right Question Strategy offers a simple proposition: schools and students would greatly benefit from parents playing an active, confident role in the development and implementation of IEPs. A parent who is unclear about the need for an IEP, unsure about what the services are meant to accomplish, and uncomfortable asking questions to clarify and understand better will not be an effective partner.

Consider, instead, a parent who understands the strategy and is able to use it to do the following:

- Play the following three roles in his or her child's education (using knowledge of the support-monitor-advocate model):
  - » *Support*—being available; attending to his or her child's basic needs; establishing expectations that school is a priority; providing encouragement for the child
  - » *Monitor*—paying close attention to his or her child's experience at school; keeping tabs on the child's daily experiences; being aware of changes in the child's feelings, performance, and attitude; noticing how the child is developing; paying attention to decisions being made about proposed strategies to help the child
  - » *Advocate*—identifying times when there is a need to speak up on his or her child's behalf; initiating contact with the school; seeking help and resources when needed; making specific requests

- Be savvy about decisions that affect his or her child's education. Being savvy begins with an ability to identify decisions and understand that any decision is the selection of one option among two or more. Then, knowing what a decision is, the parent can apply these three criteria to any decision using the Framework for Accountable Decision Making:
  » There should be legitimate *reasons* for the decision. They are based on policies, approved practices, rules, and regulations, and they are not arbitrary or discriminatory.
  » There needs to be a transparent *process* so parents can understand how a decision is made.
  » There is a *role* for parents in any decision that affects their children.
- The parent is able to
  » Produce his or her own questions about options, reasons, process, and role.
  » Improve those questions.
  » Strategize on how to use those questions.

Case Study: Support Staff-Initiated Change

The case study in this chapter demonstrates how a school-based parent liaison introduces the Right Question Strategy to a parent in preparation for an IEP meeting. The parent learns through the process about different roles she can play, how to identify decisions, and how to ask questions about those decisions. The case study focuses on the preparation before the IEP meeting and how a parent ready to play a role can help lead to a more productive partnership with the school as the IEP is reviewed, approved, and implemented. The strategy includes multiple components—the Support, Monitor, and Advocate Model (SMA), the Framework for Accountable Decision Making (FADM), and the Question Formulation Technique (QFT)—but you will see that it can be taught simply and easily.

The Letter

Ms. S grew worried as she read the note from her son J's school saying that school staff would like to start some testing to evaluate whether J should receive special education services. She didn't know how to begin to think about this. "Was there something wrong with J?" She knew he had been more reluctant than usual to go to school in the last few weeks, but she wasn't sure why. She worried that maybe there were some more problems with one kid who was bullying him last year.

Ms. S had always assumed that the school would do whatever was best. Even though she had been invited to pre-referral meetings, she didn't feel she could contribute anything, so she didn't go. Now, however, this letter was asking her to sign off on testing for "special education." The term scared her into taking action.

For advice, Ms. S turned to her cousin who told her to get in touch with Ms. R, the parent liaison at the school who had prevented school leadership from putting her cousin's child on an IEP for special needs by simply addressing some behavior problems. Ms. S remembered that Ms. R had reached out to her at the beginning of the school year, and she liked her. Ms. R was about 10 years older than Ms. S, with children already in high school. The principal had recruited her to serve in the position because she was respected by many parents. The superintendent had pushed hard along with the Title I parent coordinator for each school to have its own parent liaison who could help build bridges to parents in the community.

In Ms. R's Office

A week later, Ms. S, with her 2-year-old on her lap, was in Ms. R's office. Ms. R gave her a quick overview of the whole process for testing, creating an IEP, and determining what it might all mean. It was a lot to take in, especially since Ms. S was worrying that "something must be wrong" with J and feeling guilty about maybe having missed it.

Ms. R also told her that sometimes kids, especially boys, might get bored and begin acting out. Some teachers, especially the new ones, struggle with managing their classes, so "they try to get help, they pull in the counselor, and sometimes everything moves too quickly into referring the kids for special ed." She went on to say that both the counselor and the principal said this year that they wanted to make sure that there was a real need before any referral was made. Though this comment reminded Ms. S of what her cousin had said, she was still worried and wondered what she could do about all of this.

Ms. R then suggested that she authorize the testing so they could get to the root of the problem—if there was one. Though Ms. R couldn't be in the IEP meeting that would follow in about a month, she reassured Ms. S that the counselor who would be in attendance was very helpful, and she offered to get the three of them together to prepare for the IEP meeting during the coming weeks. Ms. R handed her some introductory information to take with her.

Introducing the Right Question Strategy

By the time she came back for the next meeting, Ms. S had read the booklet and had talked a little with her son to find out more about what's troubling him at school. He described sometimes "feeling dumb, like I don't get things as fast as some of the other kids, especially when we're reading." This was valuable information, but it only added to her sadness and fears about what might be ahead for him.

She fully expected Ms. R to start telling her what she needed to do. Ms. R, however, surprised her and said, "We're going to spend some time to give you a chance to ask some questions about an IEP."

Ms. S didn't want to be rude but said quietly, "I just want you to tell me what you know about an IEP. I don't have any other questions."

Ms. R. smiled. She'd heard that before. "I understand. I'm not keeping anything from you. I just want to make sure you feel comfortable asking questions about it. So, give me a few minutes and you'll see it's helpful. Is that okay?"

Ms. S nodded slightly, still not convinced but willing to trust Ms. R for the moment. They got started.

"OK," Ms. R got started with a smile. "Here's what I want to share with you. First, there are different roles you can play to help your child." That gave a quick shot of comfort to Ms. S who felt desperate to know how to help her son.

"Then," Ms. R continued, "I want to share with you what I learned about decisions and how that's particularly important when talking about an IEP. And, finally, I want to teach you some tricks to ask better questions so you can always do that, no matter who's in the room or who's not!"

Ms. R launched into what looked like a pretty straightforward information flow, that is, giving information to Ms. S. "Let's look first at three distinct roles you can and should play in your child's education. I have some definitions of the roles and a worksheet we can use to think about them." Ms. R pulled out a brief document that described the support, monitor, and advocate roles and began discussing them.

"The first one is to *support*. In this role, you help, encourage, and provide for your child." Before she went on, she changed the flow from giving information to asking relevant questions: "What are some things you are currently doing to support J?"

"Well," Ms. S started, "I make sure he stops playing his video games or watching TV so he can get to bed on time. I know his sleep is really important, and I try to make sure he gets enough."

"What else do you do to support him and his education?"

Ms. S was stumped. Then she perked up. "I really try to get him to eat right. It's not easy—it can cost more, even—but I try to give him good food, not junk food. And, now that I think about it, I always keep the table in the kitchen clear so he can do his homework when I'm in there."

"That's really important, all that you do," Ms. R responded. "And what do you do to let him know that you want him to do well in school?"

"I always tell him to behave and be respectful to his teacher. That's why I was really upset when I heard he was acting out and giving her trouble."

"I understand," Ms. R said, "but it's clear you are strongly supporting him at home. Now, here's another role you can play. It's about *monitoring* how he's doing—that is, paying attention and keeping track of how he's doing in school. How do you do that?"

Ms. S was silent for a bit but then volunteered, "I always ask him about how his day was, but he doesn't tell me much. I usually only find out there's a problem when his report card comes home."

"Well," Ms. R said, "by checking in with him and even by reviewing his report card, you are monitoring—you're trying to keep on top of things. It's not easy, but those are examples of you *monitoring* how he's doing.

"Here's one more role, as an *advocate*. You advocate for your son when you speak up and make specific requests on his behalf. What is an example when you have advocated for J?"

Ms. R was aware of how important it is for parents to get comfortable with the terms *support, monitor,* and *advocate* because it gives a name to the different kinds of action they take. Just getting the language gives them a new sense of what they are capable of doing for their children.

Ms. S was silent again. "Hmm, I don't know. I don't really feel comfortable talking at the school, if that's what you mean."

"You can advocate in lots of places, not just at the school. When did you speak up for your son?" Ms. R asked.

She asked it in a way that convinced Ms. S that she had indeed done it, and she quickly responded, using the language Ms. R had shared. "I advocated when another kid was looking to fight with J on the school bus. I asked the driver to pay attention to the situation, and that helped."

"There you go," Ms. R said. "You're a good advocate for your son. There are lots of ways you can advocate. Even being here trying to help yourself is a way of advocating for your son."

Ms. S smiled. It was the first smile Ms. R had seen up until then. "Let's stop for a moment and think for a second about all of the work you just did. What did you learn?"

Ms. S was now speaking more quickly and more confidently. "I see that I can play three roles. Actually, I'm already playing those three roles because I am supporting him, and I'm monitoring him—he knows that—and I guess I also advocate for him, even though I never did that with his teachers."

Identifying Decisions

"OK," Ms. R continued, "let's move on to the next thing: learning about decisions."

"Good," Ms. S spoke up. "I need to know about that."

"Decisions that affect your child's education and you are made all the time. Decisions are made at the school, district, and state levels," explained Ms. R. "There are decisions the school makes and decisions you make. There are decisions all around us, but sometimes we skip over a key thing about decisions when we're talking about them all the time."

"What's that?" Ms. S asked, again prompting Ms. R to notice that she was already proactively asking questions, signaling a change in her resolve over the course of their short meeting so far.

"People sometimes forget what a decision is. It sounds simple, but it's really important to know. A decision—*any* decision—is actually a choice to do something or to choose something over something else. Here's the definition: a decision is the selection of one option from among two or more. The option chosen becomes the decision."

Ms. S took it in but wasn't quite sure where Ms. R was going with this, so Ms. R showed her a simple page with the following instructions on it. "Think about some simple decisions you make every day—for example, the decision about what to eat for breakfast.

__cereal with milk __coffee and toast __bagel and cream cheese

"From these three options, the one you chose is the decision. If you chose cereal and milk, then that was the decision you made."

Ms. R turned the page over and said, "OK, now what are some reasons you chose one of those options?"

Ms. S said, "Well, the cereal was getting old and I thought I should eat it rather than waste it."

"OK," Ms. R said, "you had a *reason*. You always want to make sure you have a good reason behind a decision. Now, what did you think about before you decided to eat the cereal?

"I thought about how I needed to go get some more food for the house. I didn't want to buy a new box of cereal if there was still cereal in the house. But I also knew J wanted a different kind of cereal and I really wanted to make sure he had some every morning, so I had better finish this box and start with something new."

"Wow," Ms. R said, "you used a lot of information there in a really short time! You actually went through a *process* of thinking about all of that. You thought about a lot of different things, including what J wants. That's a *process*." Ms. S smiled again.

"Alright," Ms. R continued, "one last thing. You had a *reason*, and you had a *process*. What was your *role* in this decision?"

Ms. S looked confused and said so. "I don't get it. What do you mean, my role? That was all me."

"So," Ms. R responded, "you thought about someone else, about J, but still you were the decision maker, is that right?"

"That's right."

"OK," Ms. R said, "you had a reason, you went through a process, and in this case, in this decision, you were the decision maker."

She paused and saw Ms. S still looking a bit stumped.

"What do you want to know?" Ms. R's real goal was to get Ms. S to formulate her own questions, so instead of offering her the information freely, Ms. R wanted to prompt Ms. S to take the initiative and ask for information she wanted.

Ms. S said emphatically, "Why'd you do all this with me? Why'd you talk about my decision about what to eat in the morning?!"

Ms. R now shared with her a new piece of paper. It laid out clearly the definition of a decision and the three things to look for in a decision:

- The *reasons* for making it.
- The *process* when making it.
- Your *role* in the decision and the process.

"Here, this is what I just shared with you. It's called the Framework for Accountable Decision Making."

Ms. S looked at the list carefully and then raised her head sharply. "Oh, I get it! This all connects to the IEP! You want me to think about those three things when I'm at the meeting with them."

"Well," Ms. R said, "that's true, but you must also think about all of the choices considered when making the decision. You need to know that the school makes lots of decisions that affect your child, not just the IEP. It's important to be able to ask questions about all of this."

Ms. S slumped back into her chair. "I'm never comfortable asking questions at the school. Most of the time, I just feel like I don't even know what to ask."

"That's OK," said Ms. R. "I'm going to show you a way to figure out your own questions to ask."

Ms. S wasn't sure, but by now she had a lot of confidence in Ms. R and the value of what she was sharing and said, "OK! Let's try."

Ms. R showed her another piece of paper that outlined the basics of the QFT. "It's called the Question Formulation Technique. It's a way for you not only to come up with a bunch of questions but also to get better at asking good questions. The first step is to look at these four rules: (1) Ask as many questions as you can; (2) Do not stop to discuss, judge, or answer them; (3) Write down every question exactly as you asked it; and (4) Change any statement into a question. Now, what do you think might be hard for you about following these rules?"

Ms. S looked them over carefully. "Well, like I told you, I don't ask many questions, so that first one is kind of hard for me."

"Any other?"

"Well," Ms. S continued, "I kinda think when you ask a question, you want an answer right away. I don't really get why you wouldn't."

"Yeah," Ms. R said, "all that was hard for me, too, when I first started using this strategy. I also had trouble with that last one. Sometimes I thought I was asking a question, but I was just making a statement. In any case, you're going to follow these rules. Remember—I'm the enforcer," she said, laughing. "I'm going to give you a focus for your questions, something for you to ask about. Let's get started."

Ms. R presented this statement at the top of a page: *The school recommends an IEP to help your child.*

Ms. S had a quizzical look on her face. "Come on," Ms. R urged her on, "you've got some questions in you about that."

That got her started: "How's it going to help? Wait—first I want to know why he needs it."

Ms. R wrote the two questions down exactly as Ms. S had said them.

Ms. S paused and then asked in rapid succession:

- Is the IEP the same for all kids?
- Why are they saying he needs it now?
- What's different this year?
- Did he need it last year?

She paused again and looked at the list of questions with some satisfaction:

1. How's it going to help?
2. Why does he need it?
3. Is the IEP the same for all kids?
4. Why are they saying he needs it now?
5. What's different this year?
6. Did he need it last year?

Then she choked up a bit, catching Ms. R by surprise. "Is this going to make him feel stupid?" And then, after a few moments, "What can I do to help him? Oh yeah, and what will the school do so he doesn't feel bad about himself?" The questions kept coming, and the list grew.

1. How's it going to help?
2. Why does he need it?
3. Is the IEP the same for all kids?
4. Why are they saying he needs it now?
5. What's different this year?
6. Did he need it last year?
7. Is this going to make him feel stupid?
8. What can I do to help him?
9. What will the school do so he doesn't feel bad about himself?
10. Can't his teacher help him more?
11. Is there something they can do instead of an IEP?

She stopped and spent some time looking at the questions. Ms. R said, "You've got yourself a big list of questions there. Remember you said you couldn't do it? Well, you proved yourself wrong!"

Ms. S smiled.

Ms. R continued, "OK, next step. Let's take a look at these questions again and consider for a second what kinds of questions they are. Closed-ended questions can be answered with one word or a *yes* or *no*. Open-ended questions need more explanation in the answer. Can you mark the questions as open or closed?"

By now, Ms. S was stimulated by every step, and she took the pen and went down the list. She felt clear about them but wasn't sure about question 5, "What's different this year?"

In any case, Ms. R asked her to think for a moment about the advantages and disadvantages of asking closed- and open-ended questions. Then she asked her to choose a closed-ended question she wanted to make open and one she wanted to change from open to closed.

"I really want to know from his teacher what can be done to help him more. That's number 10, but now, if I ask it this way, I can see that she can have an answer on what she'll do, and I need one on what I'll do!"

"You are so right," Ms. R responded. "It really does make you think more about the answer now." She continued, "Are there questions here that connect to what we talked about before—about the roles you can play, supporting, monitoring, and advocating for your son? What about what we talked about decisions: about the reasons, process, and role? Take a look at those definitions and see what you covered in these questions."

She looked at the definitions and then back at the list of questions.

"I see that number 2, 'Why does he need it?'—that for sure is about the reason. And look at number 4 and number 5. Really, I want to know what's changed. Isn't that about the process for deciding he needs an IEP?"

She then said, "But I don't really see a question here about my role in the decision. I'm just asking what I can do to help him. I guess that's about how I can support him, but I'm worried about how he'll feel at school."

Then Ms. R suggested she look at two specific questions again:
- What will the school do so he doesn't feel bad about himself?
- Can't his teacher help him more?

"What do you see there?" she asked Ms. S.

"Well, they definitely make me want to advocate for him. Now I *know* what I want to ask in order to help him."

"OK," Ms. R said, "take these home and think about which ones you want answered before you go to the meeting and which ones you want answered at the meeting. Come back next week and show me, from all of your questions, the ones you're most eager to get an answer to."

Ms. S didn't smile. She was serious and picked up the list of questions and information sheets.

"Before you go," Ms. R said, "I want you to think about one more thing." Ms. S looked eager to hear what that was. "What did you learn from doing all of this?"

"Oh, ha. What didn't I learn? I learned about decisions, about the roles I can play, and—I can't believe it—I learned how to ask *lots* of questions."

"How do you feel?" Ms. R slipped it in as if it weren't a question she had planned to ask all along.

"I feel like now I can *do* something to help my son. I never, ever felt that before. I learned so much! Thank you!"

Then she looked worried again. "But I still don't feel like I have the answers to these questions."

"Don't worry about that right now," Ms. R said. "Now you know what you want to know, and you can ask questions. So now you'll get to work at getting answers. But not just from me. You can talk to your son's teacher. You can talk to the counselor. She's great. You'll really like her. You've got questions now, and you'll have more later. You can ask 'em!"

The Next Month

Ms. S did her homework. She had more conversations, not only at the school but also in the neighborhood. It turns out her upstairs neighbor went through the process last year and just kind of trusted the school. In that case, it worked out. "My daughter's getting more now, and I see it's making a difference."

Ms. S now felt more prepared for the IEP meeting and even a bit hopeful that it might lead to helping her son. She had started to more closely monitor his homework and saw that he had trouble finishing it. She sensed something wasn't right, but she didn't know what.

At the meeting, they shared how they came to their recommendations. They discussed the results of the testing, which revealed that there was indeed a reason J was struggling so much: he had dyslexia. They explained that condition, ways in which they were sure they could help J, and that lots of very successful people overcome dyslexia to go on to graduate from high school and college and do great things.

Ms. S had different feelings swirling inside her all at the same time. She felt comfortable realizing that there had been a full *process* and a lot of people were working on it. She also was actually relieved that there was a *reason* for J to have an IEP. It meant there was a reason he needed help, which was sure better than him not getting the help and just getting more and more frustrated. She understood the reason for the decision and the process used, but she wanted to understand better what her *role* was going to be once he had the plan. They talked about reviewing the plan, and she asked, "How will you know it's working?"

She saw that the question caught them by surprise. She actually added another one: "How will *I* know it's working?"

The counselor said, "I'm really glad you asked those questions. We're going to meet again to review how it's going, and we'll need input from everyone, including you. It will help a lot if you monitor how he seems to be doing with his work once he starts getting help."

There it was, that word: *monitor*. Ms. S said, "OK, that's what I'm going to do." Then, moving on to her perception of herself now as J's advocate, she asked, "Who do I talk to if I think there's a problem?"

There were some more looks exchanged and some hesitation until the counselor spoke up again and said, "You should feel free to always contact any of us, but J's teacher or I might be the best people to contact first."

The meeting ended. It was not easy for Ms. S. She understood J had a serious challenge, but she no longer felt alone in facing it. The very next day, she was back meeting with Ms. R, the parent liaison. Ms. S was ready to plan next steps, but first she wanted to thank Ms. R for preparing her so well for the meeting.

"Ah, I didn't do that much," Ms. R said, laughing. "I just gave some instructions and let *you* do all the thinking!"

Small Yet Significant Changes

What has changed? For the moment, only a small change. J is still facing difficult challenges, and although it is true that more resources have been mobilized to help him, a positive outcome cannot be guaranteed. It's going to be a long journey ahead.

What, then, is the significant change? J now has an advocate for life. Ms. R shared with Ms. S a strategy that is relevant not only to one specific meeting but also to J's entire journey through school.

Cognitive Changes

- *Question formulation:* Ms. S knows a process that allows her to work productively with questions as an information-gathering and problem-solving tool. For example, she knows how to generate her own questions about an unfamiliar topic. She knows the difference between open- and close-ended questions. She knows how to change questions in order to get more information. She knows how to prioritize her questions and strategize on how to use them.
- *Roles for a parent:* She is aware of three distinct roles she can play in her child's education. She knows the difference between

and the importance of each role: to support, monitor, and advocate for her child's education.

- *Decision making:* She knows how to use a framework for analyzing, assessing, and participating in decision-making processes
  that affect her child's education. She knows the definition of a
  decision and the significance of three distinct criteria for assessing a decision: the reason for it, the process for making it, and
  the role she can play in it.
- *Partners at the school:* She now understands more clearly the
  way the school operates, the different roles of various staff members, and how resources are allocated and decisions made that
  affect her child's education.
- *IEP:* As a result of all of this, she knows a lot more about the IEP
  as a process, a resource, and a specific tool for J.

Affective Changes

All of this knowledge contributes to Ms. S feeling more confident
in her ability to play a meaningful role in J's education, more hopeful
and positive about working in partnership with the school, and less
alone. She also has a greater sense of urgency that she needs to be
involved, stay informed, and speak up.

Behavioral Changes

At home, Ms. S is consciously supporting and monitoring J's
schoolwork and experience in school. She prepares questions in
advance of meetings. She becomes an active seeker of information
rather than just a passive recipient of information. She identifies
resources that can help her.

At school, she is initiating contact with different personnel,
including the teacher, counselor, special education specialist, and, of
course, parent liaison. She is speaking up, sharing information based
on monitoring J's progress, asking more questions, and seeking further collaboration.

These changes taken altogether represent a profound shift in how Ms. S sees herself and what she is capable of doing. The changes in her also have significant implications for the school and her son. The school has what it has often wished for: a parent ready and able to help her child succeed. The implications of this change, and how it came about, however, go far beyond one individual parent. The school now has a replicable strategy for working with all parents who might be going through the IEP process. The school is also tapping the full potential of its parent liaison. She proved to be invaluable. She has strong community-based connections to parents and can be a trusted resource for both schools and parents.

Ms. R was indeed an invaluable resource here, but she is not unique. There are part-time and full-time staff, paraprofessionals, and professionals working in a similar capacity in schools around the country. They can easily learn to do exactly what Ms. R did, and they can do it for individual parents as well as for groups of parents. They can share what they know and create new cadres who can pass it on to others via parent councils, PTAs/PTOs, and other peer-to-peer opportunities. All of them can become catalysts for significant improvements in the relationship between schools and families.

Parents need and deserve the opportunity to learn what Ms. S learned on her journey to become an effective partner with the school. Schools need and deserve the opportunity to engage with and partner with parents such as Ms. S. Most of all, students need and deserve adults in their lives partnering effectively on their behalf. It is a win-win-win.

5

Partnership to Increase Equity Through District-Initiated Change

The problem of disparities in achievement has bedeviled educators from the classroom to the U.S. Department of Education. It could be a group of schools in a big district. It could be just one school among three or four in a smaller district, or it could be groups of students within just one high school. The data show a clear pattern: some schools and some students within schools are not doing well. The comparative statistics are troubling and persist year after year. In addition, the problems of racial disparities often stand out since the No Child Left Behind Act of 2001 required a racial breakdown of achievement scores. The problems are painfully evident across the country:

- "On average, black and Latino students are roughly two to three years of learning behind white students of the same age." (McKinsey, 2009, p. 9)

- "Impoverished students (a group here defined as those eligible for federally subsidized free lunches) are roughly two years of learning behind the average better-off student of the same age." (McKinsey, 2009, p. 12)
- "African American students, for instance, are 3.5 times more likely than their white classmates to be suspended or expelled, according to a nationwide study by the U.S. Department of Education Office for Civil Rights." (Elias, 2013, p. 40)
- "While 82.7 percent of Asian students and 78.4 percent of white students in the class of 2008 graduated on time, that was the case for only 57.6 percent of Hispanic, 57 percent of black, and 53.9 percent of American Indian students." (Editorial Projects in Education Research Center, 2011)
- "While black students represent 16% of student enrollment, they represent 27% of students referred to law enforcement and 31% of students subjected to a school-related arrest. In comparison, white students represent 51% of enrollment, 41% of students referred to law enforcement, and 39% of those arrested." (U.S. Department of Education Office for Civil Rights, 2014, p. 6)
- Latino/Hispanic students represent 24% of student enrollment and account for 24% of students referred to law enforcement as well as 24% of students subjected to a school-related arrest (U.S. Department of Education Office for Civil Rights, 2014).

What can be done on any level—classroom, school, district, state, or national—to change the pattern? When changes occur, when the needle has moved, it is often thanks to the resolve and determination of educators at a local level (district or school) who have made it a priority and advocated for improving teaching and learning practices and for creating a school climate that directly contributes to more equitable outcomes. It's a scene played out in districts around the country: the superintendent, assistant superintendents, and principals sit around a big table poring over the results from the last round of state tests. Despite all of these efforts, how is it possible to even begin to address these challenges in a meaningful way without the active involvement of the people most affected (Minow, 2001)?

Parents' Role in District Efforts to Improve Academic Outcomes

When there are small and big crises, disciplinary or violent conflicts, or planned closings of schools, school leadership may initiate efforts to engage with and involve parents in low- and moderate-income communities, or, if they act too late, they may be responding to groups of parents that can range from concerned to angry (Auerbach, 2009).

Given the complexity of the achievement gap problem and the difficulty of finding and implementing ways to close it, it has not always been clear exactly how parents could be involved (Editorial Projects in Education Research Center, 2011; McKinsey, 2009; TC Media Center, 2005). A level of professional expertise is required to find ways to address academic problems. Parents might feel uncomfortable participating in detailed discussions of academic options. If only a few parents are invited as representatives, that number may be nothing more than token parent participation, with all of the other parents on the sidelines, not part of the process at all.

Parents simply are not expected to be part of working groups assessing and recommending specific academic interventions. Those responsibilities reasonably reside in the school's or district's domain. Where, then, can the school give them opportunities to collaborate? How can parents, if they are not architects of or partners in decision making about academic practices, still be invited into the process? That is, once invited, how can they not only feel comfortable but also have the opportunity to have their voices heard, their questions respected, and their partnership moving forward welcomed?

Building a Parent-School Partnership

In the previous chapter, you saw how a parent liaison, working with an individual parent, used the Question Formulation Technique (QFT) to help the parent ask questions about decisions that would be made at her child's Individualized Education Program (IEP) meeting and then focus her questions on the reasons, the process, and her role in that decision-making process. As a result, that parent was better able to support, monitor, and advocate for her child's educational needs.

Now we will show how the same skills—the QFT and the Framework for Accountable Decision Making (FADM)—can be used to build many parents' capacity to participate in a decision-making process focused around the issue of equity.

In this chapter, we will describe how a district and a school, as part of their overall effort to address the achievement gap, create opportunities for parents to be partners in thinking about how to help all students succeed. The case study that follows looks at a school that is doing more than making the decision about academic changes and then simply "informing" parents about it; its leaders and staff are using their commitment to achieving more equitable outcomes as an opportunity to build a strong constituency for change that includes parents. Parents who are respected enough to be fully in the loop will be better able to support the proposed changes, monitor their children's progress and communicate problems, and become advocates for all efforts to increase equity.

The school is changing the nature of its interaction with the parent community. School staff are making a special effort to give parents the opportunity to think about the problem and understand the reasons and process behind their decisions to address it. The district leadership is posing a fundamental question to the particular school making the changes: How can you involve parents in a meaningful way in a school-directed effort to achieve greater equity?

Engaging with Parents and the Community to Increase Equitable Outcomes

July

The hectic last days of the school year behind them, the members of the superintendent's administrative council convened for a three-day thinking and visioning retreat. Joining them were two assistant superintendents, the principals of all of the schools in the district, assistant principals, and curriculum specialists. The focus was on reviewing the results data from state tests students had taken the previous year. They used helpful protocols from the Data Wise Project at the Harvard Graduate School of Education (n.d.) and noticed some unsettling patterns. Among the school-based groups with some representation from the central office, one principal from a high school where students were struggling more than at other schools huddled with his assistant principal. They were concerned about the results and began to talk about what could be done differently. It was no small task. Could the school tackle the problem on its own? What changes could the leadership of the school make? And, of course, the key question: What changes would the school faculty be amenable to? They knew that no matter what they planned, without buy-in from the majority of teachers, they would be unable to make any changes.

In the last two days of the retreat, the group came up with a plan to engage faculty at their high school in a similar process of looking at the data during their first two days back at school in late August before the students arrived. They had no illusions that this was an easy nut to be cracked in two days, but they knew they'd never crack it open if they didn't create an inclusive, collaborative process with the faculty. They knew that having a deeper understanding of the problem would foster a stronger commitment to a solution that would last the entire academic year.

August

The group used those two days before students arrived to get the process started. Similar to what they had done in July, they gathered into small groups, this time along subject lines and grade levels, and used the same protocols to look at the test data. The principal then brought all of the teams back together and talked about how addressing the problem would require some decisions during the year.

"As we move through the year, we plan to use this Framework for Accountable Decision Making to make sure that we do this right, that you have a say in the decision-making process, and that we are working together in the most efficient way possible. We'll start from using a simple definition of a decision as the choice of one option among two or more options. Then we can use the three key criteria in the framework that will help us make better decisions and make the process better for all." He then presented three slides with the three criteria:

1. *Reasons:* There must be legitimate, justifiable reasons for the decisions.
2. *Process:* We want a transparent process so everyone can know how the decision is being made.
3. *Role:* There should be a role in the decision-making process for the people affected by the decision. In this case, you all, as teachers, will be directly affected by any decisions to change how we do our work to address the problem of disparities in achievement.

He gave them time to dwell on this slide—especially on item 3 about their role—and then continued. "Today is just the start. So, just as some of you do in your classrooms, we are going to start off this problem-solving process with a Question Formulation Technique. For this, we are going to move out of your current groups, sitting with people with whom you work closely, to more heterogeneous groups."

He proceeded to have different sections of the room count off and then break into new groups. Experienced in using the QFT with his administrative team for problem-solving purposes through the year, he was comfortable leading the process, beginning with a quick reminder and discussion of the rules for producing questions all the way through the reflection and next steps.

Once people formed groups and were ready to work, he got them started with this Question Focus: *Some of Our Students Are Struggling.* He then led them through the whole QFT process. By the end, there was a general consensus that they wanted to start their work on the issue during the year by looking at the following six priority questions:

1. Where does the problem begin?
2. What do we know from our own experience about what works well for all students?
3. How can we find out what methods would work best to address the problem?
4. What support will we need to make any necessary changes?
5. How's the decision going to be made about what changes we make?
6. What's our role in the decision?

Each of these questions offered them insights about what had to be done. In their first question, they recognized that they needed to understand the problem more deeply. In the second question, they asserted their own professional expertise and looked to tap into the wisdom within their ranks. In the third question, they looked outward and set a research agenda. Then, in the fourth question, they spoke from experience about the need to identify the kinds of support and resources that would allow them to make changes. In the fifth and sixth questions, they locked in on key criteria from the Framework for Accountable Decision Making the principal had presented at the outset. Finally, they wanted to know more about the decision-making process and their role in it.

There was a palpable sense of excitement as they concluded their collaborative work and broke into smaller department-based groups on the second day of the session. Many teachers talked about how glad they were to have ownership of a process to address the problem that the whole district was committed to supporting, which pleased school leadership. The process gave the teachers an opportunity to take the fall semester to articulate their own learning agenda for themselves, instead of having it imposed on them from above. This collaborative model was a great start to the new school year!

January: Where Are the Families in This Picture?

The principal, assistant principals at the high school, and department heads were meeting with the superintendent, assistant superintendents, and curriculum specialists from the central office to present the plan the school had developed with strong input from classroom teachers.

Each department, in fact, had its own plan for addressing the problem. The Math Department chair and the district's high school math supervisor talked about how the math teachers planned to change some of their teaching practices. They wanted to draw upon the successful work of Uri Treisman at the University of California and the University of Texas that has shown how students of color benefit greatly when they do more group work and group learning (Asera, 2001; Treisman, 1992; Walker, 2006). The results have been striking.

"Our teachers," the math department head shared, "are excited about this. They've been frustrated with the results and were happy to have the chance to review and choose proven, effective models that can help." They had had other thoughts on how to build more active learning into the math classes, including combining some of the methods of math educator Dan Meyer with the QFT to help students see that mathematicians "are solving problems in order to get to the next question" (Rothstein & Santana, 2011, p. 108). The English department was looking at how to promote more project-based and personalized learning opportunities so students could work independently and collaboratively on projects of interest within the current general curriculum. The history department had chosen a new framework for social studies education and its inquiry arc as a way to increase student ownership and engagement (C3 Teachers, n.d.). The science department, already committed to trying to meet the Next Generation Science Standards (NGSS) and their emphasis on inquiry, was going to deliberately foster students' ability to work with questions in science. They would expand on their use of the QFT as a core resource for helping students develop more sophisticated questions (NGSS Lead States, 2013). These solid plans, designed with guidance from the district's most important content-area experts—teachers—won over district leadership, who were enthusiastic about moving quickly to put the plans into action.

"This is amazing work," the superintendent commented. "It's clear how much the teachers feel like they can make a difference and are eager to do so. Part of that, I would guess, is that they were invited from the outset to be part of the process."

The department heads were nodding vigorously in agreement. Then the superintendent presented a challenge that caught the whole group by surprise. "We are talking about making some significant changes in how we teach. The content is pretty much the same, but how we teach, how students do their work, how they will do collaborative work, and what they are being asked to do beyond rote memorization will be changing. I think that we need to bring another group—the students' parents—into the process now. It would not be as decision makers; you and your teachers have developed good plans based on a lot of work and your expertise. But parents should be brought in now as a constituency that deserves to know what changes are taking place at their children's school."

She pointed out that although it is true that the parents of students who have struggled were certainly not leading the call for changes, that doesn't mean they are not aware of the problem. "I think it would be good to be proactive in reaching out to parents as we are trying to improve education for all students, including—and maybe especially—their children. You all have done amazing work, but you'll only be helping yourselves by making parents part of the whole effort."

The principal responded first. "We've tried to reach out to them, but we just don't get much of a response. It's not that I'm opposed to informing parents—I'm just not sure they'll be interested."

The superintendent said, "We are all concerned about the racial disparities we see here. The vast majority of our teachers are white, and the vast majority of the students who are struggling are students of color. We need to be making a special outreach effort to their parents. We need partners in supporting their children's academic work."

Listening intently, the principal began nodding his head in agreement. He respected the superintendent and got the point. His assistant principal spoke up. "I spend way too much of my 'parent time' with just a few parents of students who are being suspended or are being warned about suspension. I wish I heard from more of the other parents, especially from those whose kids are struggling. It would make it easier for me to make sure that we are all taking the issue seriously. It's harder for me if there's nobody advocating on the kids' behalf."

The assistant superintendent listened to the back and forth and then asked, "What if we tried a process with parents similar to what you did with your school staff? You all modeled a way to get buy-in for change. That's always the hardest part of a change process. Now, after getting that buy-in and more from teachers, you are recommending some changes. Doesn't it also make sense for parents to be aware of the reasons for the decision and how we made it? In addition, if they get to ask questions about it, they'll be better positioned to play a role going forward in supporting their kids and us as we make these changes."

The superintendent added, "Getting parent buy-in will be important, and we need to think about how to engage them in a meaningful way. I know that some district superintendents have made a point of 'listening' to parents' concerns, but that happens most often when there's a crisis or a difficult decision such as about which schools to close. That's fine, but we're talking about actually engaging parents in thinking with us about this difficult, longstanding challenge we are trying to address. We, as a district, have to figure out better ways to engage them as partners in addressing this 'quiet' persistent crisis."

The principal's work at his school had been validated strongly by district leadership and he came back in to the conversation and said, "I get it. We've been making a statement at our school that we all want to be accountable to one another. We can say that because we all have a stake in our success. I think the case can be made to the teachers who are working so hard on this that their job will be easier if we have parents 'on board' with our change efforts."

The superintendent concurred and said, "Remember, you are planning to teach their children in ways that are different from what they themselves experienced in school. We owe them an explanation of the planned changes."

By the end of the meeting, not all of the participants from the high school were convinced, but the assistant principal was very energized about the idea of any positive work with parents. She walked out of the meeting saying to the principal, "This is different. I really like the idea of putting energy now into using these changes—which we're doing because we want to improve the outcomes for all students—as a way to build a positive relationship with more of the students' parents." The very next day, she started working on recruiting people for a committee to work on it. Her enthusiasm was contagious and tapped into a common feeling: "I like the idea of being proactive in building relationships with parents. Too often, they only hear from us when there's a problem."

The assistant superintendent nodded and continued. "And if they get to ask questions about it, they'll be better positioned to play a role going forward, in supporting their kids and us as we make these changes."

The Plan: Reaching Out to Parents

A month later, their newly formed committee for parent outreach was working on parent invitations to a meeting about plans to improve their children's education and give them more opportunities for success. They pulled in as many people as they could to the effort, including the district's Title I coordinator, school counselors, teachers, and parent leaders. PTA leaders knew that they had had trouble getting parents involved because of the demands of long shifts at work and family needs, so they made a special outreach effort in the community, talking to friends and family, religious leaders, and some community organizations.

Their messaging led with what they hoped would be a strong hook for their outreach partners to use to get parents to come. "Come hear from school and district leaders about plans to improve your child's education. We are eager to hear your opinions. We will be joined at the event by the superintendent, the principal, staff, teachers, and community leaders."

Planning the Agenda

The committee members got to work on the event itself, but they were not sure about the best structure for it. They considered starting by letting people know about the problem that was triggering the whole effort, but that might produce defensiveness. Too many times, when parents hear from the schools, it's about "bad news." Also, starting off by talking about racial disparities might have the opposite effect of creating a collaborative working environment. The counselor, having sat in on many meetings where there was trouble afoot, piped up to say, "If we start off with the bad news, then that's going to sour the mood for the whole evening." They decided to speak positively about some special efforts the school was making to improve education for all students, and they announced that they wanted parents to be aware of the changes, to hear parents' questions, and to open up communication to help all students succeed. Mr. S, from the science department, would then lead the parents through a Question Formulation Technique, which would give them an opportunity to work on their own questions and identify what they wanted to know.

Once the parents had generated their questions, the principal would present the content of the Framework for Accountable Decision Making in a manner similar to the way it had been presented to the school staff. Then staff from different departments would share some data that had spurred them to action and outline some of the changes they would be making. They would end by answering parents' priority questions—right away, if possible—and invite parents to stay in regular contact.

Designing the Question Focus

They decided to use the QFocus as an opportunity for parents to think through the problem they were addressing and really unpack the problem with their own questions. They also wanted to explore how to change the conversation from a zero-sum game so that parents of students who were doing well would not think that by addressing differences in achievement, their children would suffer. "We have to make sure that people understand that we believe that these changes in teaching methods will improve education for all. We are moving toward a pedagogy that emphasizes 21st century skills."

Some ideas they had about a QFocus included the following:

- Scores
- All of Our Students Aren't Achieving
- We Can Do Better (accompanied by a picture of scores)
- Some Teaching Practices Will Change to Improve Education for All Students

They analyzed the QFocus examples, looking at their respective strengths and weaknesses.

- *Scores:* Simple, at the heart of the matter, but without any context or explanation, it would not work on its own.
- *All of Our Students Aren't Achieving:* This one is a valid analysis of the evidence presented by the scores, but it could be too negative. It might lead to singling out students or groups of students and could lead to some embarrassment or defensiveness.
- *We Can Do Better (accompanied by a picture of scores):* This pushes in the direction of looking at *how, we, can,* and *do better.* Lots of questions are pointed in a positive direction.
- *Some Teaching Practices Will Change to Improve Education for All Students:* This statement gets at the heart of the entire enterprise. It addresses the changes and has decisions embedded in the wording that could lead to a sharper focus on the decision making that led to the changes.

April: The Meeting

The extensive outreach efforts helped produce a larger-than-usual turnout. There were more parents of 9th and 10th graders present than 11th grade parents. The only 12th grade parents who showed up—it was near the end of senior year after all—had children in the lower grades or middle school. The principal welcomed everyone and emphasized that the entire district, from the superintendent down to individual classroom teachers, was working hard to improve the outcomes for all our students. He pointed to the superintendent who was standing on the side and welcomed her. He told the group that "she wanted to be here to listen and learn from you. We will hear from her later in the evening."

"At our school," he announced, "the teachers have really taken the lead and have been actively looking for models of teaching and learning that can benefit all students. We want to share with you tonight some of what we've learned and our plans for the year ahead, and we are eager to hear your questions. In fact, we're changing the way we usually run a meeting like this. Instead of us standing up here and giving you information and talking about what we're going to do and then asking for questions at the end, we want to begin by giving you a chance to ask questions, and then we'll start working on the answers.

"Have you ever been in a meeting where the first question comes up and you spend an hour talking about it only to realize that wasn't the right question? Does it feel like this?" He clicked on a slide that showed the face of an anguished person pulling his hair out. There was a lot of laughter. "Yeah, we've all had *that* feeling before. Well, that's what we can prevent by using a process that we often use with your children in class: the Question Formulation Technique.

"I'm going to turn the meeting over now to Mr. S, who will lead us through it."

Mr. S, the chair of the science department, explained the process. "I'll present you with a focus for your questions, you'll spend some time asking and then working with your questions, and then we'll all see which questions we can answer immediately and which ones require more research. Any question at all is encouraged. I've done this with my students many times, and even if at the beginning they're not sure what to ask, they wind up coming up with some very relevant questions and even some important ones I never would have come up with myself. So don't worry if it takes a bit to get warmed up. Your children really enjoy the process, and I hope you will, too. In fact, we use just four simple rules to help us get started asking questions." He then presented the rules:

1. Ask as many questions as you can.
2. Do not stop to discuss, judge, or answer questions.
3. Write down every question exactly as it is stated.
4. Change any statements into questions.

"At each table, you have some paper and markers. Teachers will join you at the tables to be scribes and write down all of the questions. Remember," he said smiling, "keep an eye on them—make sure they write down the question exactly as it was asked." He then asked people to briefly introduce themselves.

"Before we begin," he said, "can you talk for a moment at your tables about what might be difficult about following these four rules?" There was laughter at some tables. This quick warm-up activity gave them a heads-up how the process was demanding something out of the ordinary.

"Here's your Question Focus: *Some Teaching Practices Will Change to Improve Education for All Students*. Now, for the next three minutes, please talk *only* to ask questions about this question focus. Please limit your conversations to questions alone."

Ms. H, a U.S. history teacher, was the scribe at a table near the front. Her group looked at the Question Focus; at one another, unsure of what they were supposed to do; and then at her to get them started. She said, "I'm just here to write down your questions. Ask any question that comes to mind."

There was silence again, and then one parent got it started: "Why?" There were some murmurs and repeating of the question. "Yeah, that's right. Why?" That seemed as if that was it, and they wanted an answer, immediately. Ms. H, an experienced facilitator of the QFT process, said, "Remember the rules: we're not stopping to discuss or try to answer any question. We're just supposed to be asking as many questions as we can."

That actually got a couple more parents going. "What do you mean by 'some' teaching practices? Which ones?" There was another pause and then a parent said very slowly, "Is there a problem with what they're doing now?" And that prompted a quick follow-up question from the same parent who had started: "How do you know there's a problem?"

Then a few more parents spoke up, adding to the flurry of questions:

- Do you know that it will work better?
- Will it really work for all students?
- Is this good for our kids?
- Are they going to be behind kids in other schools?
- How will you know it works for our kids, and what if it doesn't?

Ms. H said that sounded like two questions, and she wrote them separately:

- How will you know it works for our kids?
- What if it doesn't?

After the group's initial long silence, Ms. H was having trouble just keeping up. Flashing through her head was how she'd heard many of the same kinds of questions coming from teachers when they first looked at the data, except that teachers spoke in terms of standards and testing.

Mr. S, at the front of the room, reminded them that they had only one more minute. Just as it seemed the group had no more questions to add, right at the end, one parent asked, "Do the teachers like this?" Ms. H smiled to herself as she was furiously writing down the question to beat Mr. S's deadline. "Wow, they get the whole change challenge; if teachers don't want to do it, it's not going to happen, or it's going to at least be very hard."

Mr. S brought the groups' attention back to him and showed them a slide with the definitions of open- and closed-ended questions. Take a look at your questions and find ones that can be answered with just a *yes* or *no* or one word, and then mark them with a *C* for *closed*. Then do the same for open questions—mark them with an *O*."

1. Why?
2. What do you mean by "some" teaching practices?
3. Which ones?
4. Is there a problem with what they're doing now?
5. How do you know there's a problem?
6. Do you know that it will work better?
7. Will it really work for all students?
8. Is it good for our kids?
9. Are they going to be behind kids in other schools?
10. How will you know it works for our kids?
11. What if it doesn't?
12. Do the teachers like this?

Ms. H's group members looked at the list and were sure that the first question—Why?—was open. When they got to the fourth question, they were sure it was closed. They then went through their list and saw that they had both kinds of questions.

Mr. S asked the groups to spend three minutes and name some advantages and disadvantages of asking closed-ended questions and some advantages and disadvantages of asking open-ended questions. He then talked about how both types of questions are important, depending on the kind of information being sought.

He then asked the groups to take a minute and change a closed-ended question to open and vice versa. Ms. H's group took the fourth question and changed it to "What is the problem with what they're doing now?" Then they took the tenth question and changed it slightly to "Can you know right away if it works for our kids?"

Ms. H, who knows the drill, added the two changed questions at the bottom of the list as additional questions to the original ones. Then Mr. S asked, "Choose three questions you, as a group, consider to be the most important."

Ms. H's group looked at the full list of 14 questions (now with the two questions they changed and added). By now, the group was fully engaged and comfortable contributing. "Well," one parent started, "the first one—Why?—kind of covers a lot. I think we'd want to start by knowing the answer to that."

Several parents agreed, and then one parent said, "But I think we need to know the answers to questions 8 and 14—Is it good for our kids? and Can you know right away if it works for our kids?"

Another parent said, "What if we chose number 10—How will you know it works for our kids? I think that answer would cover questions 8 and 14 also." There was some silence as the parents were taking that in and looking closely now at three different questions: 8, 10, and 14. Then a parent said, "I really want to know the answer to number 9— Are they going to be behind kids in other schools?"

No sooner had the parent made that remark that it became clear this question resonated very strongly with the group. At the front of the room, Mr. S called out, encouraging all groups not to worry too much if they're having trouble deciding. "Just choose three that are important to you so we can move on. Don't worry—your questions not chosen as priority questions won't be completely abandoned!"

There was a lot of laughter in the room and even more in Ms. H's group when one mother said, "Yeah, that's good. I was beginning to feel like you were asking me to choose a favorite child!"

Ms. H's group was adamant that the last question suggested, number 9, be listed. They also thought that the first question had to be on the list. They struggled a bit to decide but finally settled on their three priority questions:

1. Why?
9. Are they going to be behind kids in other schools?
10. How will you know it works for our kids?

The other groups in the room followed a similar pattern of silence, initial questioning, and then full-blown participation. The teachers were invaluable facilitators. Experienced in the rigor of the Question Formulation Technique, they were able to keep all groups on task.

Priority questions varied somewhat among the other groups, but they were all pretty much in the same ballpark. There were questions about reasons, questions about implications and consequences for their kids, and some questions related to teachers and the preparation needed for the changes.

For example, in the group facilitated by Mr. M, the parents first went with the global question about improving education and then circled back to the 'why' question Ms. H's group started with. They asked about the changes being made, about the decisions involved in making the changes, and about the parents' role. The process provided a remarkable window into the parents' thinking and concerns (priority questions in italics):

1. What does it mean to improve education?
2. How can education be improved?
3. *Why is the school doing this?*
4. What are the teaching practices that will change?
5. Who decides which ones?
6. How do we know the school is choosing the appropriate practices to change?
7. *Whose idea is this?*
8. Does our opinion count?
9. *Do the students know about this?*

10. When are we going to know this is working?

11. Will it be only after my kids graduate?

The teachers posted each group's questions along the walls, and the assistant principal and teachers pulled out the priority questions. They were preparing another paper with just the priority questions when the principal began to talk again.

"We're getting down the priority questions from all of the groups, and we're going to see which ones we can answer right away. Before we do that, though, I'd like to share with you a little more information about how we made this decision."

At this point, one of the parents who had been recruited by a parent leader leaned over to her and whispered, "I've been to school meetings before, but this one really is different. It's just like you said. They're sharing information about their teaching. I've never heard that before."

The principal then explained how they had used a way to look at decision making that helped make sure they were making as good a decision as possible. "I want to briefly share with you the framework we used. It's simple, but it covers a lot of ground, and you may even find that it's relevant to some of the questions you want answered."

He moved to a slide that gave an overview of the Framework for Accountable Decision Making:

- Defining and identifying a/the decision.
- The reasons for the decision.
- The process for making it.
- The role played by people affected by the decision.

Following the framework, the principal defined a decision as the selection of one choice, or option, among two or more options. He explained, "It seems almost silly that we'd have to work on that, but we've discovered that it's important to clarify just what a decision is and think about all the kinds of decisions that can be made. In this case, there were decisions to make changes, to choose specific teaching models, and to select who will be making the decision. That's why these next three criteria for good decision making are so important. Here they are."

1. *Reasons* for the decision: the basis for the decision, the justification for it, what policy or rule it is based on.

2. The *process* for making the decision: the way the decision is made, the information used, meetings, readings, discussions, and more.

3. The *role* people play in the decision: for example, which different perspectives are heard, who is involved in various parts of the process, who has the final decision-making authority.

Then he said, "Now, we'll hear from the assistant principal who has been reviewing your questions, and she'll try to answer them while keeping this framework in mind."

Ms. AP, the assistant principal, explained, "Many of the questions were about the reasons, or the basis for making these changes. This came out of conversations we first had last summer with the superintendent when we were looking at students' test scores. We noticed a pattern and saw that a good number of students here—but not all—were falling behind. We felt that we could do better and that all students in the school could do better. We got to work on it."

Then she referenced the questions that were most closely related to the process for making the decision. "You've asked about how the decision was made, including when it was made. I can tell you that we had an extensive process in which each department came up with ways they could learn and use specific teaching methods that have proven to help students who are struggling in some way. They met on their own, presented their ideas to us, and explored what additional help they would need to implement."

She then went on to the third criterion, the role played by people affected by the decision.

"The teachers were clearly the people most directly affected because they would have to carry out the changes. We knew that if they didn't feel some ownership in this, then they wouldn't be happy implementing. You asked about that—Do the teachers like it?"

The principal chimed in, "It's true that the initial push came from the superintendent," nodding in her direction, "and other district leadership, but they know and we know that this could never work if it were a top-down decision. We needed the teachers on board and feeling like this is something they wanted to do. It makes all the difference between successful and unsuccessful implementation."

The assistant principal said, "You also asked questions about two other important categories, and it's really helpful to us to think about these questions. First, I see that there are several questions about what we call *assessment*—that is, how do we know if it's working? You specifically wanted to know about how we'll know if these are the right methods."

She continued, "You also asked about *consequences*, such as 'Will our kids fall further behind?' Well, we've thought a lot about both of those, and these questions actually get at exactly why we reached out to you to come tonight."

The body language in the room was positive, with everyone listening attentively and some parents nodding in agreement and in appreciation of the acknowledgment of their questions' relevance.

"This is going to require all of us working together as we move forward," the assistant principal said. "We felt that it was, first of all, really important for you to be aware of these changes. Then, knowing what we're trying to do, you can play an important role in helping us with both of those last two categories: assessment, or knowing if it's working, and consequences, or what it means for your kids. We want to be working with you to support all students as we make these changes. As we implement changes, you should also play an active role monitoring what's happening. Keep an eye on how the changes are affecting your children. Then you can help them and us by advocating for them, or by speaking up on their behalf based on what you are observing."

She then asked the department heads to give a quick overview of some of what they were planning. "Overall," she explained, "you'll see that we are moving to an active learning experience. Students will do less sitting in rows listening to the teacher talk, and they'll be doing more hands-on work, more research, and we'll be encouraging them to ask more questions. The research has shown that this is better for achieving in school, and it will also be valuable for them in college and at work later on."

The math chair referenced research showing that students who have traditionally struggled in math benefit from doing more group work. He also noted that the same Question Formulation Technique they had just experienced would be used because "we want our students to think like mathematicians who know they need to keep asking questions in order to understand things that are difficult."

The English head talked about her teachers' goals for students to work on projects and take more responsibility for analyzing the texts they read, learning new vocabulary, and doing more writing in different forms, including reports, research papers, and essays. Ms. H quickly put up a slide that summarized a new framework that the history department would be implementing. Mr. S talked about how much of science education is moving to promote inquiry skills, or the ability to formulate questions and do independent research. "We don't want our students to fall behind, so we need to make sure that our teaching is in line with the current expectations. We also will be using the Question Formulation Technique to help students become more effective at asking questions."

The principal got up and said, "This is a lot of information. It's the result of many months of work by our teachers, and we hope that it's been informative for you. This is not the end of our conversation with you—it's just the beginning. We can learn a lot from your questions, and there still may be questions you asked that we did not get to answer tonight, but they can still be on the agenda for us to address. We are also planning to send surveys home next year to get your perspective on what you observe about how your children are working and alerting us to things we might miss.

"Right now, we'd like to take the last five minutes here for you to share in your small groups your thoughts about this question: What did you learn? The teachers will come back to the tables and take notes."

As the parents wrapped up their conversations, the principal asked if any groups would like to share with the room. In Ms. H's group, one of the parents raised her hand quickly and—after introducing herself—said, "Well, I can see how much you all have been working on this. It makes me feel good to see how much you care about how our kids are doing."

Another parent, having fully taken in the content of the Framework for Accountable Decision Making, stood up and put an emphasis on the three criteria: "I like your *reasons* for the changes you're making. It sounds like you had a good *process* in the school. And, you're *including us.* I like that!" His exclamation point at the end got a lot of vocal shouts of support and clapping.

The principal and the superintendent exchanged smiles, and both thought back to the January meeting when the superintendent challenged the group and the principal expressed some reservations. This parent's statement showed that an important constituency for change—parents—felt respected, not ignored or patronized.

A parent in another group said, "I learned that I can ask questions, that you actually want me to ask questions, and I learned tonight how to ask better questions." Another parent stood up and thanked the school but also thanked "all the parents who came out tonight, showing that we care about our kids' education. We need to share what we learned here with more parents, the ones who couldn't make it tonight. They're out there. They care. I know several who wanted to be here but couldn't."

In Mr. M's group, one parent got up, introduced himself, and said, "I wish I knew a few years ago some of what I learned tonight. It would have helped me speak up for my son, especially when he was struggling. No matter what you all do, I need to speak up for my kids. My son dropped out, but I feel that now I know better how to help make sure my daughter, my 9th grader, gets whatever help she needs."

Several other parents in the crowd were nodding again, feeling his pain and also sharing in his new confidence that he can actually advocate for his daughter. The principal thanked him for that comment and said, "There's a lot we can accomplish when we work together on behalf of your kids. Even though they're in high school and most of the time they act as if they'd prefer us—teachers and parents—to disappear, they need us. And they need us working together."

The superintendent then came up to the front of the room. A parent in Ms. H's group leaned over to the teacher and whispered, "She's one of the reasons why I came, but I forgot she was here until just now."

"This school," the superintendent started, "its leaders and teachers, and you, the parents of the students here, deserve a lot of credit. You've done something that very few schools have done. You've started a process for thinking and working together in order to improve achievement for all, and I mean all students in this school. Thank you for inviting me. I've learned a lot here and I think you all are a model for all of our other schools in the district. Thank you!"

With that, the meeting ended and the principal said, "Please, as you leave, take the cards we're handing out at the back. Each one has the Question Formulation Technique on one side and the Framework for Accountable Decision Making on the other."

The Importance of Building a Partnership for Equitable Outcomes

District leaders, school leaders, teachers, and now parents were taking on no small challenge. The district and school leaders made it clear that not only did they want parents and the community to work with them, but they respected their importance and recognized that they needed them. The parents, given the opportunity to engage and explore the problem of achievement disparity using a new kind of thinking process, bought in to the urgent need to address the problem and make some changes.

This determination to include parents and seek their support and involvement was not in the original plan. Remember, school leaders and faculty worked for months to identify the instructional changes that would begin to solve the problem. They could have proceeded without engaging parents in any way. It was, after all, the school's job and the school's right to make decisions about specific teaching and learning practices without involving parents.. There was not any immediately apparent reason to inform, much less involve, the parents.

All of that changed, thanks to one direct nudge from the superintendent. She was right. Respecting parents—all parents, regardless of race, socioeconomic status, and educational attainment—is a sine qua non for building a partnership. It is also, as she pointed out, very much in the self-interest of the beleaguered school staff. The problem is not a simple one, and there are no simple solutions. Bringing parents into the picture will not guarantee success, either, but leaving them out, the superintendent believed, will not help the school and can actually undermine the staff's herculean efforts to make changes to improve outcomes for all students.

It may not be obvious at first what parents can add to the problem-solving process, but it is critically important to tap them as resources—as partners in a student's success. The superintendent made it very clear to the district staff and principals that since parents are serious stakeholders in their children's education, they should be kept abreast of any major changes at the school. Including parents as partners in school changes gives them a more active role, transferrable skills, and a reason to participate presently as well as in the future because they are invested in the process.

Changes for the School

As this high school made clear, involving and engaging parents does not mean the school is relinquishing decision-making discretion about pedagogy. On the contrary, the proposed pedagogical changes were made without parent involvement. The changes were informed, however, by rigorous research about what teaching practices have a track record of succeeding with students similar to those attending this school. The engagement of parents was designed to strengthen a community-wide consensus for change; to create important support; and to reinforce messages to all, including students, that the school, the students' families, and the community were working hand-in-hand.

Changes for Parents

- *Cognitive:* The parents left the meeting with a better grasp of how the school was making decisions that affect their children. Sharing the Framework for Accountable Decision Making with parents makes it easy to continue to use the framework for dealing with other issues, including when new problems arise. The parents also sharpened their question-asking skills, which they could continuously use to better support, monitor, and advocate for their children's education.
- *Affective:* The skill complements parents' deeper understanding of what the school is trying to do. With this knowledge, they can

pay attention more effectively to their children's experience in school and can more readily monitor their children's progress and take note of how they are doing and feeling.

- *Behavioral:* Parents are now better prepared to speak up and advocate for their children. Their advocacy will be informed by their understanding of what the school is trying to do and by their own active monitoring of their children's progress.

Benefits

This partnership is intended to benefit all parties. The superintendent will be able to point to a new model in her district for parent engagement—a pioneering way to bring parents into a school change process and a way to create more equitable outcomes. School leaders can take pride in a consensus-building process that got buy-in and leadership from faculty. Teachers, the people who make the effort every day to give their students a chance to succeed, will see students become more engaged and more successful. Parents will value the staff's concern and commitment in a public institution working on the front lines to help their children.

As for those high school students, they now have all of the most important adults in their lives paying very close attention to their academic progress!

6

ELL Parents and Parent-Initiated Change

As previous chapters demonstrate, many actors in a school system can be catalysts for building strong school-family partnerships. From classroom teachers to district superintendents, school staff on all levels can make small but significant changes in the way they work with parents that will transform their relationships and improve collaborative problem solving for the benefit of all students.

Many school leaders, however, lament that too often they are fighting a lonely fight on their students' behalf when they try to petition for more resources and support. Teachers may turn to principals, who may turn to superintendents, who may turn to school boards, who may turn to city councils, who may turn to state and federal education officials and legislative bodies, all in the hope of securing sufficient resources to meet their students' needs. "We work with students who need additional resources," many school leaders in low- and moderate-income communities assert, "but there is no lobby representing them, no group of parents working alongside of us trying to secure additional resources. We're on our own, and we don't have much power."

The issue of equity is greatly magnified for schools serving large numbers of English language learners (ELLs) where parents may feel particularly reluctant to speak up and advocate on any level because of language challenges, lack of familiarity with the political process, and citizenship status. Schools serving communities with many low- and moderate-income and ELL parents need advocacy partners, but where are they to come from if parents are not advocating?

Traditional approaches and best practices for working with ELL parents range from ensuring communication in the parents' native language or through the use of interpreters, creating a welcoming environment, honoring cultural contributions, and building personal connections (Breiseth, Robertson, & Lafond, 2011; Hong & Anyon, 2011). Some districts commit significant resources to discrete programs to work with parents, such as Parent Universities that offer workshops a few times a year. In a few places around the country, community organizers have worked hard to create strong community-based organizations with a solid cadre of parent leaders. These parent leaders have sometimes directly challenged school districts about specific policies or practices, or they have pressured school boards, city councils, and even state legislatures to allocate more resources to the district (Berger, 2014; Mapp & Kuttner, 2013). Across the country, however, there are thousands more communities serving low-income and ELL students than there are strong, independent community organizations advocating on their behalf. The community organizing model offers a pathway to effective action, but it can be difficult to marshal the resources, time, and staffing to create sustained success.

How, then, can schools in all communities hope to generate active support and advocacy on behalf of all of their students? In this chapter, you will see how community-initiated use of the Right Question Strategy can lead to a strong initiative to address critical issues and provide essential support for school leaders in a time of crisis, demonstrating that this strategy can help educators not only take proactive steps to reach out to parents (as we've done in previous chapters) but also recognize and seize opportunities to respond effectively to parents and community leaders who approach them, making the most of these contacts to create a solid foundation from which to build positive, effective partnerships. Though the partnership in this chapter's case study doesn't start with the school, the outcome, as in earlier chapters, is the same: a stronger partnership grounded in parents' capacity to participate effectively in their children's education. Parents become active participants and advocate for important new resources, and school leaders come to fully appreciate the value of this new partnership, especially in finding new ways to collaborate with community-based programs and services.

An Overlooked Resource: Community-Based Human Service Agencies

For too long, schools have been asked to take on the challenge of educating students with great needs, with a shrinking pool of resources. Daily problems and occasional crises in students' lives outside school affect their experiences in school. Schools need additional voices speaking up to meet the needs of ELL students. In our work, we have learned of a greatly overlooked resource in communities with large ELL student populations, be they in remote rural areas, densely populated small and large cities, or peripheral towns and districts: human service agencies. These organizations constitute an enormous infrastructure with the potential to build parents' capacity for partnership and ability to advocate for the needs of ELL students. Almost all communities include case workers, social workers, ESOL and adult literacy instructors, youth program staff, early childhood educators, and neighborhood and faith-based program staff who are in regular contact with ELL parents—and thus perfectly positioned to build parents' capacity to partner with schools and advocate for their children (Jackson & Turner, 2015). Human service agencies are an invaluable resource for engaging parents of ELL students for three key reasons:

- They are part of an already existing infrastructure of services and programs. A school does not have to do any additional work to create new organizations, pay for new personnel, or secure additional resources.
- The staff working in these positions often have earned the trust of ELL parents who look to them for advice and support on a range of issues, from housing, employment, health care, and education.
- They are experienced working with parents in a supportive role and often recognize that the parents need to learn self-advocacy skills.

This network of community agencies is typically eager to play a role in building ELL parents' capacity once they have learned to use and teach the Right Question Strategy.

The Underestimated Potential of ELL Parents as Advocates for Education

Once the Right Question Strategy is shared in community settings, a new layer of leadership, initiative, and advocacy begins to take root. Parents who learn the Right Question Strategy often become strong leaders in advocacy efforts. They do not, however, see themselves as traditional leaders who "speak on behalf of the community." Rather, the Right Question Strategy is perceived as something to be shared with all, not reserved for only a few who get leadership training. Parents often feel a sense of urgency to take action but lack specific skills to do so. They are, nevertheless, quite capable of levels of agency that can lead to substantive improvements for their children. In other words, not only can they support and monitor; they can also advocate.

In this chapter's case study, you will see precisely how a staff person from an outside agency can be a catalyst for bringing ELL parents into efforts to address their children's needs. The agency point person focuses on building parents' capacity to ask questions; focus on key decisions; advocate for more resources; and lobby and hold accountable a school board, a city council, and other decision makers who affect their children. Very quickly, the agency staff person becomes a resource on the side while parents who have never been heard from before, including some who have never crossed the threshold of their children's school, start to shape and lead an advocacy effort that demonstrates just how valuable a resource they are for their own children and the school. Parents move from not knowing how, where, and by whom decisions are made to becoming active participants in shaping a decision-making agenda on many levels.

Case Study: A School Shooting

Four worried parents were sitting in E's home. The day before, a 12-year-old had come to school with a gun from home and, somehow—it's not clear how—shot another student. These parents had gathered in E's home because they trusted him and looked to him for guidance. He worked for a human service agency that provided a range of programs, educational workshops, and services for new parents, for parents of children with special needs, and for any parent in the largely low- and moderate-income community who needed help navigating different systems and services.

E didn't have a lot to tell them. This was a pretty serious problem— well beyond the general health, education, and services information he was accustomed to giving. It wasn't clear how he could help them, but it was clear they needed help.

He said, "Right now, this is a pretty difficult situation, and I'm not sure what to do about it, but I think before we jump too quickly to take action with the first idea that comes up, we could actually spend some time figuring out what questions we need to ask."

It made a lot of sense to E but not to the parents. E saw the confusion and frustration on their faces and said, "OK, I really think this can help us figure out what to do. Give me only 15–20 minutes."

The parents nodded their willingness to try. E, knowing that he barely had 15 minutes, moved quickly into the first step and simplified the rules for producing questions, shortening them to just one.

"OK," he started, "I'm going to present to you what we're going to ask questions about. I'm going to say it and then, no conversation about it, you just ask questions. Try to ask as many questions as you can. Is that clear?" he asked. They semi-nodded again, still unsure what this was all about.

He presented the Question Focus: *A Shooting at Our Kids' School.*

The father sitting next him spoke first, saying, "They have to do something about this!"

"Oh, man," E thought, "*that's* why there's that rule about changing any statements into questions. Now, I'm in this position where I have to correct him; that will just be confusing and make him feel bad, and he may stop participating."

E wrote it down and said gently, "I wonder how we could take that statement and turn it into a question." The father looked confused, but his neighbor spoke up and said, "What are they going to do about it?"

Everyone nodded confidently. They sat there for a moment in silence. It was as if they already got to the main point. "What are *they* going to do about it?"

E was sweating the silence though tried not to show it. The first question, the seemingly all-encompassing first question, suggested that this was something for somebody else to take care of, for somebody with some power. In these immigrant parents' eyes, that was the school, a place many of them had never even entered.

More silence. Then E said, "Look at the statement again. What more do you want to know? What other questions do you have about A Shooting at Our Kids' School?"

"What are they going to do to make sure it doesn't happen again?"

Again, E noticed, a question about *they*. Then someone with a child in 7th grade said, "Are the police involved?" This was quickly followed by "Are our kids in danger?" This provoked another question about the students: "Will more kids start bringing guns?"

Then the questions moved to parents: "Where are the parents of this kid?" "Did they know their kid was bringing a gun to school?" These questions led them into a new direction: "Is the school going to tell us what they plan to do?"

"Yeah," responded the father who had started with a statement. E thought it was going to be another statement, but he was wrong. In the flow, the father asked, "Is there something we can do to make sure they tell us?"

The parents' body language changed. It was as if his question drew their attention to something that had not been on their radar screen when they began this process: *the idea that they could take action.*

E sensed that they were ready to move on and didn't want to miss the opportunity to build upon this initial round of questions. He quickly invited them to look at the list of questions he had written down and see which ones could be answered with just a *yes* or *no*. He read each one out loud.

1. They have to do something about this!
2. What are they going to do about it?

3. What are they going to do to make sure it doesn't happen again?
4. Are the police involved?
5. Are our kids in danger?
6. Will more kids start bringing guns?
7. Where are the parents of this kid?
8. Did they know their kid was bringing a gun to school?
9. Is the school going to tell us what they plan to do?
10. Is there something we can do to make sure they tell us?

They saw that six out of the nine questions could be answered with a single word. "I learned that those questions," E explained, "are called closed-ended questions. The questions that can't be answered with *yes, no,* or one word—and need more explanation—are called open-ended questions."

He didn't have much time to look at which ones they could practice changing, as the next step in the Question Formulation Technique called for. Instead, he asked them to look at questions 9 and 10. "Let's try to change those into questions that require more in the answer."

One of the group offered, "Do they have to tell us what they're planning to do?" The neighbor spoke up and said, "That still is a *yes* or *no* question."

They slumped a bit and looked again at the questions. E helped out with a few hints. "Well, open-ended questions often begin with the words *what, why,* and *how.*"

They sat back up and now looked closely at the questions. Suddenly, a parent asked, "What can we do to make sure they tell us?"

E added the two new questions, the closed one and the open-ended question, to the list. "¡Sí, sí!" three parents responded. The last question cracked open a window they had not been aware of before, one that included a role for them to play.

"Here's the final step in this process," E started. "Choose the three questions you think are most important."

They gathered around the list and looked closely at all of their questions. They debated for a while—about the police, the shooter's parents—and then came back to the most pressing question that was foremost in their minds: Are our kids in danger? Once they had that, they added two open-ended questions:

- What are they going to do to make sure it doesn't happen again?
- What can we do to make sure they tell us?

They selected three priority questions and wrote the numbers of the questions in the sequence:

3. What are they going to do to make sure it doesn't happen again?

5. Are our kids in danger?

12. *What can we do to make sure they tell us?*

All of this took 25 minutes, not the 15 E had promised. No one noticed or complained. A new, strong energy filled the room, and E wanted to make sure they had a chance to reflect. He said, "Before we finish this process, it's important to think about this question: What did you learn?"

There was silence, but not the awkward kind from the beginning of the process. It was a "thinking silence." E, the skilled facilitator that he was, sat comfortably and waited for them to speak. Then the neighbor said, "I didn't think I'd be able to ask any more questions after that first one. It felt good to be able to ask all of those questions. It helped me think about what I really wanted to know."

Her friend said, "I never thought about how you ask a question can make a difference about the kind of information you get." Then a fourth parent, who remained the most reticent to participate, said, "Yeah, and that last question gets me thinking more about what *we* need to do."

E asked them to see where in the list their priority questions come from. They laughed a little when they saw 3, 5, and 12 out of 12. "That's really something," the neighbor observed. "From near the beginning, the middle, and the very end. And that one at the end wasn't even on the first list!"

Then the fourth parent, who had remained the most reticent to participate, said, "Yeah, and that last question gets me thinking more about what *we* need to do." His comment produced vigorous nods in agreement. One parent's face lit up, and she said, "We need to do this with other parents. A lot of parents are upset and don't know what to do. This could really help. How can we get them to learn it?"

The meeting now had one item on the agenda. Before any of them would try to address the problem, they knew they needed more parents involved. How could they make that happen?

They moved into a discussion about how they'd recruit more parents, where they could hold a bigger meeting, who would run it, if E would be able to lead the process with all the parents, and how they could help, now that they'd gone through it. The group, which an hour earlier hadn't been able to imagine coming up with a few questions, now had lots of them.

The group of four reached out to more parents and asked for help reaching out to the community. Their message was clear: "We need more parents to help us do the kind of thinking we've done already. If they don't start asking their own questions, they'll just be following us. We need their questions, too."

A week later, the worries about their children's safety were still strongly felt throughout the community. Thanks to a handful of parents' work with door-to-door and telephone outreach, they estimated that 150 parents might show up for the emergency meeting to be held in a church basement.

E was impressed by the response. The night before, he had recruited three other staff members from the agency who knew the Right Question Strategy to meet with the original group of four parents to talk about how they would facilitate the process with such a large number. The original group of parents brought along a few other parents so that they would understand more about the process.

They decided that E and M, one of the original group of parents, would be up front to lead the process and give instructions as the parents moved through the steps of the Question Formulation Technique. Depending on the final numbers, they would split up into groups, use some flipcharts E's agency made available, and work with each group on their questions. "The small groups will need you all to help keep them on task," E explained. "It's going to be a new experience for all of these parents. They may feel as uncomfortable as you felt at the beginning. You can help them feel more comfortable, but you need to stick with the process to make it work for them just as it did for you.

"Here are the most important points to keep in mind in your small groups. We are going to use four rules for producing questions and have parents think about what might be difficult about following them. Then we present the QFocus: *A Shooting at Our Kids' School*. They need to ask their own questions. Make sure they follow the rules. If they start talking or making statements, remind them of the rules.

"Remember, though, this is about them asking their own questions. They may want you to tell them or give them examples, but it's going to work better if they have to do the thinking themselves. We'll keep it moving, giving instructions about when to move on to the next steps. As they go further along in the process, you'll see that they'll really start thinking!"

The Emergency Community Meeting

The parents had set the time of the meeting for 7 p.m. but knew that not all people would be there, arriving only after they got things settled at home. Some came with young children in hand. The youth group at the church was recruited to take care of the youngest kids.

At 7:15, they began. There were 100 people in the room. M and E welcomed everyone and went over the plan for the meeting. E explained, "We can't solve this problem tonight, but we need to think together about what we want and what we think the school should be doing."

He then asked them to break up into small groups. E and M circulated around the room, checking in on the groups as they got to work. In the group where M's neighbor was leading the process, they had some trouble beginning, but she encouraged them by saying, "It's OK not to know the answer now."

The lists of questions began to grow. For example, Group 1 began with questions similar to those the group had come up with at E's house.

1. Why did it happen?
2. Are our kids in danger?
3. Can't the school keep our kids safe?

Then the questions went in a slightly different direction, asking for some history.

4. Has the school ever had a shooting before?
5. Is this connected to the fights that go on there?

Their questions began to zoom in on their kids, the student who did the shooting, and his family.

6. Can we promise our kids that they'll be safe at school?
7. Was there something wrong with the kid who did it?
8. Where are his parents?

There was a lull at that point, which E noticed also occurring in a few other groups. He called for everyone's attention for a moment and said, "There are a lot of questions being asked and we're about to do some more work with them, but before we do, ask your last questions. Maybe you want to think now about next steps. What do you want to ask?"

This seemed to pump new energy into the groups. One father asked, "How can this be prevented?" Next, a mother asked, "Can we help the school?" That one triggered a couple more questions as the parents were getting really comfortable asking: "Is the school going to keep this from happening again?" "Are they doing something right now?" Then one parent added a final question: "What can we do?"

Group 2 developed their questions in a similar way. However, these parents zeroed in a bit more on who was involved in making the decisions and getting information.

1. How safe are our children at school?
2. Why did this happen?
3. Is the school helping our children deal with it?
4. What are they going to do to make sure it doesn't happen again?
5. How do we keep ourselves informed of what the school is doing?
6. Who else is worrying about this?
7. Is the school going to tell us what they are doing about it?
8. Who is going to decide what to do?
9. Is there a way we can make sure something's done?

E and M then gave instructions for the groups to go through the process of looking at closed- and open-ended questions, changing them, and prioritizing them. Group 1 went through the process of changing questions and understanding what happens when you change a question. They went, for example, from "Can't the school keep our kids safe?" to "What are they going to do to keep our kids safe?"

The groups then chose their priority questions and shared them with the room. E and M asked the small groups to think about what they learned from their own questions and from other parents' questions. In Group 1, a father said, "The other group asked about who's deciding. I never thought about that, but I guess we need to know that."

That question about who was going to decide next steps wound up being a top-priority question for the whole crowd. When they talked about what they wanted to do now, a strong consensus was that they wanted to present the priority questions from all of the groups to the principal and get him to answer them. They agreed to type up the questions and send them to the principal; then, to make sure that he understood they wanted answers, they were going to request that he meet with them the following week to answer their questions.

M asked them to discuss in their small groups, "Before you leave, please share with one another what you learned tonight." As she walked around the room, she heard reflections similar to what her small group had shared just a week earlier. She heard discoveries about how much you can learn by asking questions and by changing questions from one type to another. She heard another lesson that her group had missed: "I'm glad we asked 'Who's going to decide?' We need to know that."

Preparing for the Meeting with Leadership

The principal was surprised to get a request to attend a meeting with parents, especially one to take place in the community. After years of sparse attendance at parent nights at the school, the last thing he expected was for a group of parents to request his appearance at a community meeting to discuss their list of questions.

The invitation was an interesting turning of the tables, and he valued it. For years, he had struggled to secure resources for teachers who were charged with the challenge of working with largely first- and second-generation immigrant children, from homes where only Spanish was spoken and there was a reticence to get involved in any way in their children's education. He wasn't sure what to expect at this unusual meeting. He feared that the parents might have expectations that he alone had the final say in response to all of their requests or demands. He knew that the answers to these questions required input from people above him in the decision-making hierarchy, and he wasn't about to go to a meeting if all he could tell parents was "Go talk to somebody else."

After discussions with some staff at the school, he responded to the request, saying that he'd be glad to attend but that the superintendent and school board members should also be invited.

E met with a group of parents and relayed the principal's response. This triggered a series of new questions from a group that was now more than comfortable asking questions:

- The problem is at the school. Why does he say he can't do what he wants? He's the principal.
- What does the superintendent have to do with this?
- What do the school board members do?
- Why should they be there?
- Is he not going to come if the others don't come?
- How do we get them to come?

One of the parents who worked as a custodian at the central offices shared that she likes the superintendent, who would always greet her and ask her how her children were doing. She encouraged the group to follow the principal's advice and invite the superintendent.

The superintendent agreed to come. It was more complicated for school board members because if they all came, certain open-meeting laws would need to be followed. There was no disagreement that this was a serious issue, and they recognized that if parents were requesting a meeting, especially parents who rarely participated, it would not be good to refuse it. The school board chair and one school board member would attend and report back to the whole school committee.

The parents' analysis of who needed to be present, how many could be present, and, especially, why district and elected officials should be there uncovered the multiple layers of authority within a system educating their children. This was no small revelation for many of the parents in the room, some of whom were citizens, some with green cards, and some who did not fall into either category. Not more than two or three had ever voted, and no matter their citizenship status, only a handful had ever been involved in their children's school. Having already crossed an international border at one point in their lives, it was as if now there was a foreboding and impenetrable wall—another *frontera* of its own—between them and the public institution and democratically elected officials charged with educating their children.

One parent said, "I always thought the principal was like the boss, but I see now the principal's more like my supervisor at work, and he's got to report to people further up." Another parent shared, "Well, I always thought the superintendent was the boss, and I never thought about the school board before."

Introducing Parents to the Framework for Accountable Decision Making

The group had already achieved unprecedented success by demanding and getting the full attention of the district's decision-making hierarchy. There was a danger, however, that with all of the different levels of authority that would be gathered in the room, the language, jargon, bureaucratic complexity, and political posturing might undermine the great power of parents who had tried to set an agenda. Indeed, they were setting the agenda literally and figuratively. Not only would they determine who would speak and in what order (parents first!), but they also set high expectations that whatever needed to be done could be agreed to at the meeting.

"There's so much positive energy coming from the parents," E shared with colleagues. "If they come and get the run-around, I don't know what's going to happen. I'm worried." One of his colleagues suggested, "Why don't we see if we can gather some parents together the night before the meeting and share with them the decision-making framework we learned at the training? I didn't fully get how important it was until after the training, and I started to pay closer attention to how decisions are made all around me—at work, even at the health-care center. It's going to be really relevant for when all of the district and school board people start making comments or responding to the parents' questions."

They managed to recruit a good number of parents to a prep meeting with the pitch that, "Now that there are more school district people coming, we've got to be ready for all of them." E and his colleagues promised that it would be a quick but important meeting.

The night before the big event, they met and got right to work. E started by saying, "When we first got together, we used the Question Formulation Technique. It really helped get a lot of important questions out and helped us plan and get this meeting. Tonight, we want to share one more thing we learned that we think is going to help us tomorrow night. It's also pretty simple but helps you see things you might miss. I'm going to start with something that might make you wonder what the heck I'm doing, but give me a minute." By now, there was an even stronger bond among E, his colleagues, and the parents in the room, with a lot of trust going both ways.

"Think about what you prepared for dinner last night."

There was some laughter in the room. "My son doesn't like it when I make tacos with mushrooms instead of pork," one mother shared, "so I made it only with pork."

"That's helpful," E responded. "So, you were thinking about two different choices, one was tacos with pork and the other was tacos with vegetables. That's really what a decision is—selecting one thing among different choices, or options."

The parents nodded. It seemed to make sense, and they all recognized this simple definition of a decision: the choice of one option when you have two or more things you can choose from.

"Now," E continued, "why did you choose the pork?"

"It's like I told you," the mother said. "My son won't eat tacos unless they have pork. That's why."

"OK," E said. "So that was your reason. You had a reason for the decision to make tacos with pork. It's not like you didn't think about it. You thought about it before making the decision and you had a good reason for it."

He continued, "Now, before you made the decision, before you chose which option, what else did you think about or do?"

"I told you. I thought about what my son will eat. Well, I guess I also thought about what food was in the house. Oh, now that I think about it, I also thought about how I didn't have much time after getting home from work, so what would be the fastest."

Her unpacking of all that she was thinking about just to make dinner got another mother thinking out loud. "Oh, yeah, and I better check what I have in the refrigerator. You may want to make the tacos with pork, but if you ran out yesterday, you can't do it!"

That brought more laughter, and E observed, "So you actually had to think about a lot of things even in making that decision. Not just what your son likes, but also how much time you had to prepare the food and, also important, what food you had in the house. That's a lot of things to keep track of. You may not always see that you do a lot of thinking every day before coming up with a good reason to make a choice—you know, to make a decision. That's what you did."

This comment produced more knowing nods and some real interest, as E went on to say, "Here's one last thing I want you to think about. Who made the decision? Who chose to make tacos for dinner?"

"Was it my son," the mother asked tentatively, "because he wouldn't eat it the other way?"

The other mother chimed in, "You knew what he wanted, but it was still you making the food. You chose what to do. You could have chosen not to prepare what he wanted."

Another parent seconded that, and E said, "You made the decision. You had a role in this decision. In fact, you made it. But before you made it, you thought about different things, you went through a few steps—a process. You used information, listened to different people, like your son, and only then you made a decision.

"That's an example of a decision where you can make it. But in lots of situations where other people are making decisions, it can be hard to figure out what our role is in that decision making. What we learned about decision making means that no matter when a decision is made, we need to know a few things."

E then shared the criteria for good decision making:

- The options that were or should have been considered.
- The reason(s) for a decision.
- The process for making the decision, including the information used.
- The role you got to play in the decision. Even if you're not a decision maker, did the decision maker know what you wanted or what you were thinking?

The group had turned serious, and before E segued to the meeting the following evening, the first mother spoke up. "Oh, now I see why you wanted to know what I cooked for dinner. If we want to make sure the school makes good decisions, we need to know all of that—the reason, the process, and our role."

"And don't forget we need to know what choices they're making," chimed in the second mother.

The two women were on the case and basically took over the leadership from E. He had hoped this would eventually happen, but he was excited to see how they were connecting all of the dots so quickly.

In fact, the first mother, M, took the words out of his mouth, "We better be ready to ask questions about all of that tomorrow!"

One of the fathers, also feeling more confident now that he was armed with the Framework for Accountable Decision Making, spoke up. Although E did not use that term, the parents gave it their own name, the Decision Rules. The father said, "We need to use these Decision Rules to check the questions we prepared for tomorrow night."

They reviewed the list they had created:

1. What are they going to do to make sure it doesn't happen again?
2. Are our kids in danger?
3. What can they do right now?
4. What can we do to make sure they tell us?
5. Who is going to decide what to do?
6. Is there a way we can make sure something's done?

They noticed that their questions were mostly about asking the school to do something and to give the parents some information. Because they were thinking about options, they really liked the one that started, "What are they going to do . . . ?" The parents would now be much better prepared to listen to the answer to that and other questions and be ready to ask about other options.

Using their Decision Rules, they also looked at their questions differently. The questions were the same, but they understood them differently now. They liked that they had a question about making sure the school kept them informed. They were now hungry for more information so "we can make sure we know about what they are doing."

They did, however, want to add more questions.

- What plans does the school have to prevent situations like this?
- What options do they have?
- Who will be involved in finding what to do about it?
- Who will be deciding about what to do and by when?
- How will the solution be chosen, and based on what?
- What will be our part in it?

They finalized the agenda, making sure that their priority questions would be center stage, and they reviewed the plans for making sure to get as many parents there as possible. E asked, "Who's going to manage the meeting? Who's going to open it?"

"Won't you?" asked one of the parents.

"Nope," E said. "You've done all the thinking about what you want to say and what you want to ask. All I did was just share a couple of tools with you." E knew that it was really important to break the pattern of dependency, to show people how much they are capable of figuring things out for themselves if they have the right tools.

Quickly, the group chose the father in the first group to open the meeting, welcome everyone, and keep the meeting on schedule. They wanted M to present the questions to the school administration.

They also did something interesting that took the strategy beyond where E had led them. "Let's make sure," the second mother said, "that those of us here are actually thinking about more questions when the school officials start to talk."

"Yeah," said one father who hadn't said much before. "We can use these Decision Rules if we need to ask them about decisions."

They dispersed quickly to get home, leaving eager for the meeting and confident about themselves. E and a colleague lingered a bit and thought about how quickly the parents got the Framework for Accountable Decision Making. "Yeah," said E, "they got it more quickly than I did, for sure." His colleague said, "I think that's because we were trying to imagine how to use it. It was like a thinking exercise. But, for them, they didn't have to imagine anything. They know now what they need to be paying attention to. It all made sense to them, and that's why they could take it and run with it so quickly."

The Big Meeting

There was a large turnout. The parents had placed chairs up front for the two school board members, superintendent, and principal. Next to them was an easel pad with the parents' priority questions prominently displayed. The school board members huddled together to look at the questions, pointing to one after another while talking about them. The first responses to the parent questions came from the school board chair.

The parent who had thought that the superintendent could do anything she wanted whispered to E, "I guess this means he's the one giving the answers. That shows that the superintendent isn't really the big boss."

The school board chair explained that they all shared the parents' concerns about the violence at the school and, addressing their question about the safety of their kids, talked about how it's a priority for the district that all students be safe at school. "That's why," he continued, "the superintendent and I are talking to the mayor and the chief of police about getting a police officer assigned to the school."

He went on to say that, of course, they would keep the parents informed and that they would be doing everything possible to prevent this from ever happening again. He described other things the schools were trying to do and encouraged the parents to give their children the strong message to be safe, not cause problems at the school, and work hard.

His comments were not appreciated. "What does he think we're saying to our kids now?" E overheard one parent saying quietly to another. "To misbehave and *not* work hard?" The other parent responded in a louder voice, "A few kids cause some problems, and they want to blame all of us!"

The father chairing the meeting asked if parents had any comments or questions after the school board chair's comments. This unusual timing caught the school officials by surprise. The parents had decided to change the dynamic of the meetings from a "question-and-answer" portion, in which just a couple of people might dominate with their own questions, to this new format so that more questions and perspectives could be heard.

A parent raised his hand and thanked the school board chair, adding that he agreed there should be more police presence at the school. He then asked what the school was doing to prevent the fights that have been happening. "Nobody's talking about those fights because nobody's been shot before, but my kids are scared sometimes that there's going to be another fight."

One of the mothers who had been part of the organizing group followed and said, "Our kids need something to look forward to, not to be afraid of. One of my cousins said that at her kids' school, they have after-school programs, and the kids know that if they get into trouble, they can't attend them. That keeps them in line."

The chair of the meeting now turned to the school officials, who turned to the superintendent and the principal, requesting their responses. The principal leaned over to the superintendent to say something and then stood up. "We're trying to work with the kids who are getting into fights," he said. "When we have to suspend kids, we do, and we bring in their families. We're dealing with that. Also, we'd like to offer more after-school programs, but some kids, your kids, live far away and there's only one time the buses can go. We don't have any other options."

When he mentioned the word *options*, some knowing looks were exchanged in the audience; this was a word that now had more meaning to the folks who had been in the prep meeting the night before. In fact, one of the parents from that meeting asked, "Why can't they do a late bus run for the kids who want to stay?"

The superintendent then stood up and said, "Well, that's just not an option we have available to us right now. All these things we're talking about cost money we don't have. The after-school programs, the extra transportation so your kids can attend then, training programs to work with the kids to reduce the fighting, even getting a police officer there cost money we don't have. We just don't have any more funds in this year's budget."

M moved to the front and asked, "Who decides how much money you get?"

E exchanged knowing looks with his colleague before noticing that several of the other parents turned around to him with the same intent, smiling because they knew exactly what M was doing.

The school board chair began to talk about different funding sources—federal funds, state funds, and funds from the city council. M followed up by asking, "But who decides how much money you can spend?"

This question gave them pause, and the school board chair and the superintendent exchanged looks to see who would answer. After a brief pause, the school board chair got up and said, "Well, I guess that's the city council. I mean, we present them with a budget request and ask them to approve it, but they've got the final say."

M was now climbing further up the public decision-making hierarchy, but she was worried because she sensed they were just passing the buck. One of the parents asked, "Well, will you actually do these things if there's money for them?"

This question gave them all pause. This was a sharply pointed, closed-ended accountability question, pure and simple, being asked of them in a very public setting. They hesitated, but then the school board member who had not spoken up to that point said, "We'd actually have to get the approval of the school board for any changes in the budget, and that's not simple. We need to look at the school's budget, the transportation budget, and more. We'd also need a plan from the superintendent and the principal about their plans for staff training and for after-school programs."

The parent didn't back down. "If they do that, will you ask the city council for money?" Another simple, clear, closed-ended, powerful accountability question—a question for which it would be hard to answer with a simple *no*. The parents had not only shaped the agenda in advance of the meeting, their questions were now setting an agenda for what these public and elected officials needed to do after the meeting.

The superintendent kept emphasizing that they couldn't make this change happen overnight. "There are things we do that the state department of education requires of us, including how we use our time in school," he said. "We might need approval if we make changes to use time for violence prevention programs. We might have to apply for funds from them to do that. They might even have to request permission from the federal government's Department of Education."

The school board chair added, "We can present anything we want to the city council, but they'll probably tell us that we could do them only if the state legislature approves more funding for schools."

Additional decision-making bodies, distant and well out of sight beforehand to the parents, were now introduced by the people the parents previously had assumed had the authority to make any needed changes in the school. The situation was getting more complicated.

"I feel like you're giving us all sorts of reasons why not much is going to be done," said M. By now, her voice was strong and she was getting a lot of support from the crowd. "We're not going away, and we're going to make sure that something gets done, something more than the one option you gave us—to get a police presence on site. There are more options, and we're going to keep pushing for them."

This meeting with parents was different from anything the school officials had experienced before. The meeting had been called by the parents. They set the agenda. Their questions determined what was discussed. They were using language that had not been heard before, discussing options, asking accountability questions, and raising expectations that the officials were working for them and were expected to get what was needed for their students—no matter how many approvals were needed.

M concluded by saying, "Before, we were kind of asleep. We weren't paying attention to any of this—not the school board, not the city council, and definitely not anything at the state or federal level. But no more. We are going to pay close attention to these authorities, and we're going to keep asking questions until we get the answers we need."

From a Public Event to Positive Outcomes

The parents gained new confidence about their ability to hold public officials accountable. They perceived the differences between officials who seemed genuinely interested in getting the resources and making the needed changes and those who seemed more intent on giving them the run-around because it was just all too complicated. The parents kept at it.

E continued his involvement, but now, he was only needed on the side and occasionally in an educator's role. For example, he shared with the group the full name for what they called the Decision Rules. He said, "It's not important what you call it, but here's the way I learned it. You can see it has the word *accountable* in it. And that is exactly what you all have been doing. You've been holding people accountable by using the Framework for Accountable Decision Making."

The city council soon saw an entirely new population of observers and participants in public forums. The majority of the council seemed determined to oppose any changes in the budget. That soon changed because the parents kept pushing. Somehow, money appeared fairly quickly in the school's budget for violence prevention and after-school programs. Another late bus run was added, and the climate at the school improved.

Just after they had secured funds from city council, one of the city councilors most sympathetic to the parents' cause told one of the parents, "Other city councilors started calling your group *La Fuerza* [The Force], because we didn't know what hit us. You came out of nowhere, and you're making people do things they never thought of doing before. If you keep it up and start voting, you'll really make an even a bigger difference."

A few months later, E ran into a woman who had come to all of the meetings but had never said anything. She told him, "You know, after we went through all that, all those meetings, I started to think a lot more about my kids' education, and I began to pay more attention to what they were bringing home. I noticed that my 4th grader, well, he always got his homework done much quicker than my 6th grade daughter and even faster than my son who's just in 2nd grade. I asked my 4th grader how come he finished so fast, and I didn't get much out of him. But it seemed strange to me, and then I saw his report card, and I wasn't happy about his grades. So I sat down and took myself through that process—you know, asking questions—and I prepared a bunch of questions for the teacher. Then I did something I've never done: I asked the teacher for a meeting. Well, we met and it turns out that she's worried about him, too, and was glad that I asked to meet with her. She's going to see if he can get some extra help, but she told me to keep an eye on how he's doing and that she'll keep me posted, too. You know, I never could do something like that—actually ask questions of a teacher. It feels good. It feels like I can help my son even if I didn't finish high school."

A year later, the school board had a new member. It was M, the mother who had so quickly connected the dots between what she cooked for dinner and the decisions in the public arena. With support from others in *La Fuerza*, she ran a campaign more about continuing the education—the investment E had made in the initial group—and less about herself as the person who would be the problem solver for the community. She said, "I want to get elected not to speak for you, but to speak with you and alongside you. If we are going to make changes, we need more people up there speaking out and making their voices heard."

The Great Potential of a School-Community Partnership

Communities around the country have many examples of new "heroes" who emerge and rise up out of nowhere in a time of crisis, which can create a kind of spontaneous combustion of energy that opens up an opportunity for community mobilization on a new level. M could have easily been one of those new, powerful leaders who went on to represent parents in her community, to be an authentic voice speaking up for them.

She was, however, a very different kind of leader—not the hero but the facilitator who helped other people continue to think and grow and take action alongside her. She understood that one leader cannot solve the problem. She and other members of *La Fuerza* understood that the more people asked questions, the more actual decision makers would listen and respond. The role of M and her fellow community residents was to insert themselves into the decision-making process, to create a role for themselves, even when it is not clear where or how that can happen. Their roles were not just to support and monitor but also to advocate. They knew they could always hold public officials accountable with their new strategy for developing thoughtful questions.

The story here is about how schools can benefit from previously overlooked resources in the community. Too often, staff at underresourced schools "tend to displace the responsibility for skill learning on the parents or the students themselves" (Edmonds, 1979, p. 18). For this reason, they don't invest in parents the way E did, helping them develop their ability to think for themselves, represent themselves, advocate for themselves and their children, and hold decision makers accountable.

This idea of a specific "investment" in parents is evident in the work of various school staff in every chapter of this book. In this chapter, a social service agency and a frontline worker became an invaluable source of social and political capital that were critically important for schools working with a large number of parents who were not accustomed to making their voices and needs heard in circles of power.

Changes for Parents

Cognitive

- Parents became aware of the importance of asking questions to explore a complex issue.
- They realized that there was a need to reach out and get more parents to ask questions.
- They learned that the schools could not do the work alone and that they could work alongside them as advocacy partners with their children's school, to lobby for the funding and resources necessary to make real change.
- They learned about a decision-making hierarchy and became more sophisticated advocates after initially not even being aware of any level of decision making at their children's school higher than a teacher or the principal.

Affective

- Parents felt confident in their ability to ask questions of decision makers.
- They also felt that they had the ability to take action and hold decision makers accountable.

Behavioral

- Parents reached out and engaged other parents in an advocacy effort.
- They mobilized to advocate more effectively with decision makers.
- They asked priority questions they had produced and asked additional ones.
- They held decision makers accountable at different levels, including the school committee and city council.

Changes for Organizations

- The agencies became a resource for building parents' skills for participation.
- The agencies now have a strategy they can integrate into their work to help people help themselves. (E did not ask them questions to get them thinking. He taught them how they could figure out their own questions. That's what they did: they asked the questions and connected the dots.)
- There are far more social service agencies serving larger numbers of parents and families than there are community organizing efforts. Social service agencies in a community have various state and federally funded contracts to work with parents of children with special needs. They are embedded in the community and are often places where parents feel comfortable. This is an example of how these resources can be tapped in a way that benefits the parents, the school, and the students.
- Parents participating in community organizing efforts and parent leadership programs have also used the Right Question Strategy to make valuable contributions to building strong partnerships. The Right Question Strategy can be a resource for all programs working with parents (Ferlazzo & Hammond, 2009; Sexton, 2004; Warren, 2001).

Benefits for the School

Before the first meeting, teachers and school administrators believed they were on their own trying to help students, address a crisis, and lobby key decision makers for more support and resources. Once the community moved into action, the school had stronger allies than ever before to help address both a crisis and students' long-term needs. This is no small accomplishment. School staff, as well as parents, often feel overwhelmed by the enormity of the challenges they are facing. When they create a new partnership that includes collaboration with human services agencies, they are building a model of a more holistic approach to improving educational outcomes.

Benefits for Students

The benefits for students were, on one level, quite tangible: increased after-school activities, additional bus service, and the marshaling of resources to provide violence prevention education in the school. On another level, students had an alliance behind them that had not previously existed. School staff, agency staff, parents, community members, and individuals higher up the decision-making chain were now all focused on giving students what they needed.

A Model for Building a School-Community Partnership

In communities around the country, adult literacy instructors, social service caseworkers, social workers, youth program staff, early childhood educators, community organizers, and neighborhood advocates are perfectly positioned to share the Right Question Strategy with immigrant parents. They are on the front lines, working daily with people far removed from power who believe they do not have a say in decisions that affect them and see no way to play a role.

The story of E, M, and the parents in the community who became *La Fuerza* reflects a larger story of how agencies and parents in a low- and moderate-income community, and particularly immigrant parents, can become an invaluable resource for schools trying to meet the needs and deal with the crises that come up in their students' lives (Ferlazzo & Hammond, 2009). By seizing every opportunity to build the capacity of all parents to support, monitor, and advocate for their children's education, schools—especially those serving poor, immigrant, and often marginalized communities—can help level the playing field and break the cycle of disadvantage.

Conclusion

One main story plays out in different ways throughout this book: *Educators and parents in low- and moderate-income communities, facing a wide range of serious challenges, use a simple strategy to build a strong partnership on behalf of all students.*

What is this story's significance? Certainly, one part of its larger meaning is connected to how it was done. Educators could use the Right Question Strategy as part of their ongoing work, without requiring additional personnel, resources, or funding. Parents could learn the strategy in a variety of settings and on different levels, with opportunities to internalize what they learned; reflect on its importance for their efforts to help their children succeed; and put it into practice immediately and repeatedly.

Implementing the strategy did not require a major new programmatic initiative or a large infrastructure in order to deliver and learn the strategy, nor did it ask parents to take a "crash course" in the content of what their children are learning or the intricate details of how a school and school system work. The strategy, in fact, is deliberately kept simple, accessible, and free. It teaches just two key skills that are essential and invaluable for parents to use throughout their child's education from early childhood through high school:

- The ability to formulate questions, improve those questions, and strategize on how to use them.
- The ability to participate effectively in decisions that affect a child's education.

The actual significance of what educators and parents do in this book, however, goes well beyond the mechanics of how they learn the strategy and how to use it. There are outcomes that point to a transformation in their relationship and in the ways they take action:

- *Agency:* The parents, by learning to use just two skills effectively, transform themselves into active agents confidently working on behalf of their children. As Bandura (2001) states, "To be an agent is to intentionally make things happen by one's actions ... rather than residing as a discrete entity in a particular place. The core features of agency enable people to play a part in their self-development, adaptation, and self-renewal with changing times" (p. 2). Parents move from feeling disengaged, fearful, and incapable of playing any role in their children's education to becoming agents on their children's behalf, working in new ways to *support* their children's education, *monitor* their progress, and *advocate* for them when necessary.
- *Partnership:* School staff and the key adults of a student's life come to see how they are invaluable resources for one another and for the student. We are also expanding the possibilities of partnership to delineate a more holistic approach that includes the important role human service agencies can play in building capacity for people they serve to participate more effectively in their children's education.

The new sense of agency demonstrated by parents reflects major *cognitive* changes as they gain new knowledge and new skills; meaningful *affective* changes as they come to feel more confident and a greater sense of urgency to participate; and long-lasting *behavioral* changes as they take action in strategic, more productive ways at home, at school, and in the community.

Investment Leads to Agency, Which Leads to Partnership

Throughout this book, the people who were the catalysts for the changes that led to strong partnerships made an initial commitment to teach and share two seemingly ordinary skills. The skills for asking questions and participating in decisions, however, are anything but ordinary. Indeed, they are quite sophisticated ones that are traditionally held and used by people with more power, knowledge, and authority.

The actions in the case studies presented here demonstrate a willingness to share the power of the skills and an understanding that no one was "giving up power" but, rather, was sharing something powerful that could help them all achieve common goals. The teaching of the skills began with professionals—an individual teacher, a parent liaison, school and district leaders, a social service staff person—and was eventually taken on by newly engaged parents who taught the skills they had just learned to other parents. The professionals and parents were modeling how to democratize access to skills that enable more effective action and stronger partnerships.

In their work with parents, the educators in this book are implementing a form of "democratic education," as John Dewey (1916) might have described it had he seen it in action a century ago. Public school staff members who use the Right Question School-Family Partnership Strategy are helping to create examples of what we call a "microdemocracy," in which individuals can participate effectively in decisions that affect them in their interactions with public and publicly funded institutions. The parents with whom they work begin to activate important democratic habits of mind and practice as they become more skilled in asking their own questions and participating in decision making. The parents are not "empowered" by anyone else but rather use these robust skills to analyze, assess, plan, strategize, collaborate, participate in decisions, and take effective action.

We must make it easier for educators and parents in struggling communities to use the essential skills outlined in this book to make democracy work for them. We need all hands on deck in order to address the causes and contributing factors of inequality outside school walls—as well as the disparities in outcomes within them.

It can be done. It requires a commitment to invest in more people. We have presented a simple, free way to do it. Teach parents two skills that help them play three roles—support their children's education, monitor their progress, and advocate for them when needed. The outcome is strong partnerships that lessen the burden on educators to do everything on their own and make it easier for parents to play an active, constructive role in their children's education.

This book is our modest contribution to creating those partnerships. We expect that once you start to implement the strategy in your schools and communities, the results will be anything but modest.

The Right Question Strategy meets parents where they are and makes a direct investment in their ability to participate in their children's education, recognizing that "no system, no individual dealing daily with large numbers of people can meet all their needs without the avid involvement of those whose needs are to be met" (Minow, 2001). As parents learn the skills for more effective participation, they become more determined to play an active role, as this one mother living with her children in a homeless shelter in Louisville, KY, made clear.

As a result of this workshop I plan to: _What ever it takes to get the information I need._

We look forward to continuing to learn from parents like her and to continue learning from you as you demonstrate new ways to use and adapt this strategy for building school-family partnerships and for creating more equitable educational opportunities for all students. As public educators, you will be making yet another contribution to building a more just and inclusive democratic society.

Appendix A
Resources for Further Reading

Introduction

Coffman, J. (2002). The Right Question Project: Capacity building to achieve large-scale sustainable impact. Retrieved from www.hfrp.org/family-involvement/publications-resources/concepts-and-models-of-family-involvement

Chapter 2: Partnership Through Teacher-Initiated Change

Flamboyan Foundation. (2011, July 29). Teacher family engagement resource: Building relationships with families. Retrieved from http://flamboyanfoundation.org/resources-and-publications/

Flamboyan Foundation. (2013, February 13). Parent teacher conferences resource tools. Retrieved from http://flamboyanfoundation.org/resources-and-publications/

National Center for Quality Afterschool. (2015). The afterschool training toolkit: Homework Help. Retrieved from www.sedl.org/afterschool/toolkits/about_toolkits.html?tab=homework

Spelling, M. (2005). *Helping your child with homework*. Washington, DC: U.S. Department of Education, Office of Communications and Outreach.

Walker, J. M. T., Hoover-Dempsey, K., Whetsel, D. R., & Green, C. L. (2004). *Parental involvement in homework: A review of current research and its implications for teachers, after school program staff, and parent leaders*. Cambridge, MA: Harvard Family Research Project.

Chapter 3: Partnership Through School-Initiated Change

Center for Safe Schools. (2014). Pennsylvania bullying prevention toolkit. Retrieved from www.safeschools.info/content/BPToolkit2014.pdf

Parent Teacher Association. (2016). Connect for respect—bullying. Retrieved from www.pta.org/programs/content.cfm?ItemNumber=3003

PrevNet. (2015). What parents need to know. Retrieved from www.prevnet.ca/bullying/parents

Reform Support Network. (2014). Strategies for community engagement in school turnaround. *Reform Support Network*, 1–24.

Weissbourd, R. (2014). Making caring common. Retrieved from http://mcc.gse.harvard.edu/

Chapter 4: An IEP Partnership Through Parent Liaison–Initiated Change

Katz, B. (2013). The collaborative IEP: How parents and teachers can work together. *Special Education Guide*. Retrieved from www.special educationguide.com/pre-k-12/individualized-education-programs-iep/the-collaborative-iep-how-parents-and-teachers-can-work-together/

Smith, L. (2003). Parental participation: Collaboration in the IEP process. *William & Mary School of Education: Training and Technical Assistance Center*. Retrieved from https://education.wm.edu/centers/ttac/resources/articles/familyinvolve/pp_iepprocess/index.php

Stanberry, K. (2014, January 29). Playing a role in the IEP process. *Understood: For Learning and Attention Issues*. Retrieved from www.understood.org/en/school-learning/special-services/ieps/playing-a-role-in-the-iep-process

Staples, K., & Diliberto, J. (2010, July/August). Guidelines for successful parent involvement: Working with parents of students with disabilities. *TEACHING Exceptional Children, 42*(6). Retrieved from http://tcx.sagepub.com/content/42/6/58.extract#cited-by

Chapter 5: Partnership to Increase Equity Through District-Initiated Change

Agronick, G., Clark, A., O'Donnell, L., & Stueve, A. (2009). Parental involvement strategies in middle and high schools in the Northeast and Islands Region. *Regional Educational Laboratory: Northeast & Islands.* Retrieved from http://ies.ed.gov/ncee/edlabs/regions/northeast/pdf/REL_2009069.pdf

California Department of Education. (2014). *Family engagement framework: A tool for California school districts.* Sacramento: Author. Retrieved from www.wested.org/wp-content/files_mf/1414600912familyengagementframework2.pdf

Connecticut State Board of Education. (2003). *Revised position statement on school, family, and community partnerships.* Hartford: Author. Retrieved from www.sde.ct.gov/sde/LIB/sde/pdf/board/SFCP.pdf

Davis, D. (2000, June). Supporting parent, family, and community involvement in your school. *Northwest Regional Educational Laboratory.* Retrieved from www.pacer.org/mpc/pdf/titleipip/SupportingInvolvement_article.pdf

Kirp, D. L. (2013). *Improbable scholars: The rebirth of a great American school system and a strategy for America's schools.* New York: Oxford University Press.

Smith, J. (2006). Parental involvement in education among low-income families: A case study. *The School Community Journal, 16*(1). Retrieved from www.adi.org/journal/ss06/SmithSpring2006.pdf

Velsor, P., & Orozco, G. (2007, October). Involving low-income parents in the schools: Community-centric strategies for school counselors. *Professional School Counseling, 11*(1). Retrieved from http://professionalschoolcounseling.org/doi/abs/10.5330/PSC.n.2010-11.17

Wagner, T., & Dintersmith, T. (2015). *Most likely to succeed: Preparing our kids for the innovation era.* New York: Scribner.

Westmoreland, H., Rosenberg, H., Lopez, E., & Weiss, H. (2009). Seeing is believing: Promising practices for how school districts promote family engagement. *Harvard Family Research Project: Issue Brief,* 1–16.

Chapter 6: ELL Parents and Parent-Initiated Change

Campbell, L. (2012). Facilitating change in our schools. *Creating the Future.* Retrieved from http://education.jhu.edu/PD/newhorizons/future/creating_the_future/crfut_campbelll.cfm

Rabinowitz, P. (2015). Changing policies in schools. *Community Tool Box.* Retrieved from http://ctb.ku.edu/en/table-of-contents/implement/changing-policies/school-policies/main

StopBullying.gov. (2012). *Community action toolkit.* Retrieved from www.stopbullying.gov/prevention/in-the-community/community-action-planning/community-action-toolkit.pdf

Warren, M. R. (2001). *Dry bones rattling: Community building to revitalize American democracy.* Princeton, NJ: Princeton University Press.

Appendix B
Materials for Facilitating the Right Question School-Family Partnership Strategy

This section offers guides and materials for teaching the Right Question Strategy to groups and individual parents. It includes annotated facilitation guides for each one of the components of the strategy, handouts and worksheets for parents, and planning templates.

The full Right Question Strategy can be integrated into your work with individuals and groups of parents. The strategy is designed to allow for a modular approach. There are many ways to mix and match the three components. The components can be used as standalone activities or in combination. The materials in the annotated guides will help you teach parents how to ask their own questions, how to focus their questions on decisions, and about three roles they can play.

Objective

Introduce parents to all of the components of the Right Question Strategy:

- Asking questions using the Question Formulation Technique.
- Participating in decisions using the Framework for Accountable Decision Making.
- Playing three roles for partnering in their children's education: support, monitor, and advocate.

Process

Facilitating the full strategy is divided into three distinct activities:

1. Facilitating the Question Formulation Technique (QFT).
2. Asking Questions about Decisions: The Framework for Accountable Decision Making.
3. Three Roles Parents Can Play: Support, Monitor, and Advocate.

Facilitating the Question Formulation Technique (QFT)

Time: 15 minutes with individuals; 45 minutes with groups
Handouts: Question Formulation Technique Summary; My List of Questions to Ask

Process

1. Introduce and discuss the rules for producing questions.
2. Introduce the Question Focus.
3. Ask participants to produce questions, categorize and prioritize questions, discuss next steps, and reflect.

Producing Questions	Facilitation Tips
Introduce the Process Let participants know that they will be working with questions and the specific purpose. Tell participants you will be giving a focus for asking questions, or Question Focus, but that first there are some rules to review and discuss.	The introduction should be brief. You want participants to get to work quickly. Make sure there is a clear goal for asking questions. Examples can be preparing for a specific meeting, planning, or problem solving. The goal can also be one for educational purposes to familiarize participants with the process for asking questions.
Introduce and Discuss the Rules Rules for Producing Questions: • Ask as many questions as you can. • Do not stop to discuss, judge, or answer the questions. • Write down every question exactly as it was stated. • Change any statements into questions. Ask parents to name what might be difficult about following the rules.	The rules provide a structure on how to produce the questions. The rules describe how individual parents and groups are expected to work. Do not skip the discussion of the rules the first time you introduce parents to the process. You can also ask, "Which one of the rules will be most difficult for you to follow?"
Introduce the Question Focus Say, "Our focus for asking questions is _____."	Just present the Question Focus. You don't need to explain it or give any additional information, but you may ask, "What questions do you have?" or "What would you like to ask?"

Producing Questions	Facilitation Tips
Ask Participants to Produce Questions Ask participants to produce as many questions as possible, following the rules, and number the questions.	Make sure participants understand the task at hand. They are asking questions about the Question Focus (statement, picture, problem) you presented. Clarify for participants whose perspective they are taking in: "You are a parent," "You are a community member," and so on. Parents may write down their questions, or you may serve as the scribe for the group. Repeat the instructions if parents are struggling to produce questions. Try your best not to give examples of questions. Some participants may feel as if they are already asking questions or that they know what questions to ask. If this happens, let participants know that the process can help them improve the questions they are asking.

Improving the Questions	Facilitation Tips
Categorizing Questions Define closed- and open-ended questions. Ask participants to • Label closed-ended with a C. • Label open-ended with an O. Ask them to name advantages and disadvantages of asking closed-ended questions. Then ask them to name advantages and disadvantages of asking open-ended questions. Finally, ask parents to practice changing questions from one type to the other.	Closed-ended questions can be answered with *yes* or *no* or with one word. They often start with *is, do,* or *can.* Open-ended questions need an explanation. They often start with *why, how,* or *what.* Discuss one type of question at a time. If participants have difficulty categorizing the questions, practice labeling together one question of each type by checking how it will be answered: "Can this question be answered with *yes* or *no* or with one word? If so, it is closed-ended; if not, it is open-ended." Name advantages and disadvantages of each type of question. Changing a question from closed to open and one from open to closed will be sufficient for practice.

Prioritizing Questions	Facilitation Tips
Choosing Priority Questions Ask participants to choose priority questions, keeping the Question Focus in mind.	Say, "Choose the three most important questions from your list. Let's mark them with an *X*." An alternative can be to ask parents to choose the three questions they would like to address first. The goal is to familiarize parents with the idea of prioritizing. The number of priority questions can change depending on the number of questions produced. For example, parents might choose one priority question from a list of three.
Discussing Next Steps	**Facilitation Tips**
Ask parents to discuss and/or strategize on their role in the next steps.	Think ahead of time about how the questions will be used. Are you answering some of the questions? Will the questions be used as a learning agenda? Will the questions be used as a guide to communicate with parents? Think about what to do with parents' questions. What information should they get, and what steps need to be taken? The goal is for the parents to know there is a clear plan to implement.

Discussing Next Steps	Facilitation Tips
Sharing Out When the QFT process is used with groups, it is good practice to share out the work before the reflection step.	You may ask participants to share the questions they changed from closed to open and from open to closed, their priority questions and the rationale for choosing them, and the next steps to be taken with the questions.
Reflecting	**Facilitation Tips**
Ask parents to think about the following: • What did you learn? • How can you use it?	Ask parents to respond to one question at a time.

Tips for Supporting Facilitation

Make sure that participants know the plan, timeframe, and purpose for the session (i.e., why are they asking questions or asking questions about decisions?). The goal when facilitating the Question Formulation Technique is to ensure that participants are producing, improving, and prioritizing their own questions.

For the Facilitator

- Do not give examples of questions.
- Do not interrupt the process to answer questions.
- Make sure the group stays on task as they generate questions. This is a new way of working, and they may fall back into talking rather than posing questions.
- Remind the group to follow the rules. For example, participants may talk rather than generate questions or not write down the question exactly as it was asked.

- You may serve as a recorder—for example, when time is limited, there are literacy issues, or the parent is more comfortable doing the thinking but not writing.
- Validate all contributions equally by simply saying thank you.

QFT Sample Facilitation Timeframes

The timeframe for asking questions using the QFT can be adjusted depending on the time available. For example, when working with individual parents, you will be able to cover all of the steps in about 15–20 minutes. There will be situations where time is even more limited, but such times could also serve as opportunities for practicing the question formulation skill. When time is limited, you may skip some of the steps in the process. Make sure to provide support materials for parents to practice the full Question Formulation Technique process.

Question Formulation Technique with Individual Parents: Sample Timeframe

Process	15 Minutes	7 Minutes
Producing questions: • Introduce purpose of process. • Discuss or introduce the rules for producing questions and present the Question Focus.	5	4
Categorizing questions	3	—
Prioritizing	3	2
Discussing and strategizing next steps	2	—
Reflecting	2	1

You can facilitate the QFT with groups in a variety of timeframes, such as a 30- or 40-minute workshop. The process can also be used with groups in both longer and shorter timeframes.

Question Formulation Technique with Groups of Parents: Sample Timeframe

Process	30 Minutes	40 Minutes
Producing questions: • Introduce and discuss the rules. • Introduce the Question Focus. • Produce questions following the rules.	8	10
Categorizing questions	5	6
Prioritizing	5	6
Discussing next steps and sharing out	8	12
Reflecting	4	6

The Question Formulation Technique (QFT)

Produce Your Own Questions
Use a *Focus* or *Question Focus* to ask questions about, and follow the four essential rules for producing your own questions: • Ask as many questions as you can. • Do not stop to discuss, judge, or answer the questions. • Write down every question exactly as it is stated. • Change any statement into a question.
Improve Your Own Questions
Think about two types of questions: closed- and open-ended. • *Closed-ended questions* can be answered with *yes* or *no* or one word. • *Open-ended questions* require an explanation and cannot be answered with *yes* or *no* or one word. Categorize questions as closed- or open-ended. Find closed-ended questions, and mark them with a *C*. The other questions must be open-ended, so mark them with an *O*. Name the value of each type of question: • Advantages and disadvantages of closed-ended questions. • Advantages and disadvantages of open-ended questions. Practice changing closed-ended questions to open-ended and vice versa.
Prioritize Your Questions
Choose your three most important questions. Think about why you chose these three as the most important.
Strategize On Next Steps
Think about next steps. What information do you still need to get? What tasks do you need to implement?
Reflect
What did you learn? How can you use it?

Question Formulation Technique Worksheet

My List of Questions

Question Focus/Topic: _____

Date: _____

1. Ask as many questions as you can about the topic.

• Do not stop to try to judge or answer the questions.

• Write each question exactly as it comes to mind.

• Change any thoughts or statements into questions.

2. Find different types of questions.

• Closed-ended questions can be answered with a *yes* or *no* or with one word.

• Open-ended questions require an explanation.

3. **Practice changing questions to get different information.** Change one of each.

Closed → Open	Open → Closed

4. **Choose the three most important questions from the list.** Mark them with an *X*.

5. **Name the next steps you will take with the priority questions.**

6. **Reflect:**

Asking Questions about Decisions: The Framework for Accountable Decision Making

Time: 60 Minutes

Handouts: Question Formulation Technique Summary; Framework for Accountable Decision-Making Summary; Asking Questions about Decisions Worksheet

Process:

1. Define the term *decision.*
2. Provide examples of everyday decisions.
3. Introduce and define key elements in decision making: reason, process, and role.
4. Instruct participants to produce questions about decisions using the Question Formulation Technique.
5. Ask participants to prioritize questions about reason, process, and role.
6. Ask participants to reflect.

Process	Facilitation Tips
Define the term *decision* and provide examples of everyday decisions.	
A *decision* is choosing one option from among two or more. *Example:* decisions about what to eat for breakfast: From these three options, the option that you choose is the decision. When decisions are made, there should be options to choose from. Ask participants to name an example of a decision they made.	The goal is not to go deep into decisions but to provide a working definition. Do not skip defining what a decision is. Use simple daily examples that participants can relate to. Make sure participants understand the idea of options and have them think about a decision they made today.

Option A	Option B	Option C
__ cereal & milk	__ coffee & toast	__ bagel & cream cheese

The decision to _____.

Introduce and define key elements in decision making: reason, process, and role.	
The Reason "Reason" should help explain or provide a basis for the decision—information used, policies, standards, regulations, etc. Ask participants to name the reason for the decision, and make them aware that there are good reasons for their decisions.	Breakfast example reasons: • Food available • Wanted to have something different than the previous day
The Process "Process" helps explain how the decision is made—the steps taken, meetings held, protocols used, place, time, and people involved. Ask participants to name the process for making their decisions, and make them aware that there is a process when they make decisions.	Breakfast example process: • Checked what was available • Thought about breakfast the day before
Your Role "Role" is the part you play in the process. Ask participants to think about their role in making the decision, and make them aware that they had a role in the decision.	Clarify that there are decisions in which other people are the decision maker—they have a role. There are many decisions that other people make where there should be a role for the people affected, such as supporting the decision, giving input, or advocating. They can also play an active role by asking questions.

Facilitating the Question Formulation Technique (QFT)

Time: ~11 minutes for individuals/one small group; ~18 minutes for a large group working in small groups

Process

1. Introduce and discuss the rules for producing questions.
2. Introduce the Question Focus.
3. Ask participants to produce questions following the rules, and categorize them.

Producing Questions	
Introduce and discuss the rules for producing questions.	Facilitate a discussion of the rules if this is the first time participants are experiencing the QFT. Review the rules otherwise.
Introduce the Question Focus.	The Question Focus must include a decision.
Ask participants to produce questions following the rules, and categorize them.	When using the QFT in combination with the Framework for Accountable Decision Making you can use the first three steps of the process for participants to produce and categorize the questions. The prioritization step is optional.

Asking Questions about Decisions

The prioritizing step of the QFT is optional. Asking questions about decisions boils down to the following main steps:

1. Identify questions about reason, process, and role.
2. Ask new questions in any missing areas.

Asking Questions about Decisions	
Identify Questions about Reasons Ask participants to review the list of questions they produced and try to find a question that will help them learn about the reason for the decision. If they don't have a question about the reasons, they should ask a new one.	Participants should not spend a lot of time trying to make questions fit into the category. You might need to remind participants that they are looking for a question that will help them learn about the basis for the decision (e.g., information used, policies, standards, regulations).
Identify Questions about Process Ask participants to review the list of questions they produced and try to find a question that will help them learn about the process for making the decision. If they don't have a question about the process, they should ask a new one.	If needed, remind participants that they are looking for a question that will help them learn about the steps taken; meetings held; protocols used; or place, time, and people involved.

Identify Questions about Role Ask participants to review the list of questions they produced and try to find a question that will help them learn about their role or the role of the people affected by the decision. If they don't have a question about their role, they should ask a new one.	Remind participants, if needed, that they are looking for a question that will help them learn about their own role or the role of the people affected by the decision.
Reflect Ask participants to reflect on two or more of the following questions. Introduce one question at a time. • What did you learn? • How/Where can you use it? • What value do you see in asking questions about the reasons? • What value do you see in asking questions about the process for making the decision? • What value do you see in asking questions about your role? • What could happen if you ask questions about the reasons and process but not about your role?	Make sure to budget the time for the reflection. This step helps participants internalize what was taught. Participants can reflect individually and then share in small groups or as a large group.

Sample Facilitation Timeframes

The timeframe for this activity can be adjusted based on time available. Note that the timeframes are approximate. They are samples of the minimum time you will need to facilitate the Framework for Accountable Decision Making and the Question Formulation Technique. If you are working with one small group to produce and identify questions about decisions, budget 30 minutes; if you are working with several small groups, budget 50 minutes.

Framework for Accountable Decision Making Combined With QFT: Sample Timeframe

Step	30 minutes	50 minutes
Defining a decision	3	4
Exploring key elements: reason, process, role	3	7
Asking questions using the QFT • Introduce and discuss the rules. • Introduce the Question Focus. • Produce questions.	7	11
Categorizing questions	4	7
Prioritizing	Optional	Optional
Identifying questions about reasons/ adding new ones	3	5
Identifying questions about process/ adding new ones	3	5
Identifying questions about role/adding new ones	3	5
Reflecting	4	6

FADM Tips

The goal when facilitating the FADM is for participants to become aware of the concept of decisions and ask questions about three specific criteria for accountable decision making.

- Participants need to understand the differences between reasons, process, and role. The facilitators should be ready with simple daily-life examples to quickly show the differences.
- The goal is to identify questions in all three areas (i.e., reason, process, role). Participants may try to find a question that encompasses everything. Make sure they find a question for each.
- If participants and facilitators disagree on the category of a question, facilitators should instruct groups to provide a rationale for the categorization.
- Participants may have trouble categorizing questions from their list. If they can't quickly find a question that fits a category, then they should produce a new one. The facilitators need to be ready to give instructions about producing a new question.

The Framework for Accountable Decision Making and the Question Formulation Technique

Defining a Decision
A decision is the selection of one option from among two or more options.
Exploring Three Criteria for Accountable Decision Making
Things to know in any decision that affects you: • The *reason* for the decision—the basis for the decision. • The *process* for making the decision—steps taken, by whom, where. • The role—the part you play in the decision-making process.
Asking Questions about Decisions
Use a topic or Question Focus to ask questions about decisions following these rules: • Ask as many questions as you can. • Do not stop to judge or try to answer the questions. • Write down the questions exactly as they come to mind. • Change any statements into questions.
Categorizing the Questions
Categorize your questions as closed- or open-ended.
Identifying Questions about Reason, Process, and Role
Review your list of questions to find questions about the following: • The reason for the decision. • The process for making the decision. • Your role in the decision-making process. If you can't find a question about any one of these three criteria, ask another question.
Reflecting
What did you learn? How can you use it?

The Framework for Accountable Decision Making Worksheet

Learning How to Focus on Decisions		
What is a decision? A decision is choosing one option from among two or more. *There are options. The option chosen becomes the decision.*		
Name an example of a decision you made today:	Name two options you had. Then check the option chosen. __ Option A: __ Option B:	
What were your reasons for choosing option ____?	What was your process for choosing?	Were you the sole decision maker?

Asking Questions about Decisions

Question Focus:

Produce questions. Follow these rules: Ask as many questions as you can. Do not stop to judge or try to answer them. Write the questions exactly as they come to mind. Change any thoughts or statements into questions.

Categorize your questions. Identify closed- and open-ended questions. Label closed-ended questions with a C. Label open-ended questions with an O. Change questions from one type to the other.

Asking Questions about Decisions

Find one question about the reason for the decision. If you don't have a question about the reason, come up with a new one.

Find one question about the process for making the decision. If you don't have a question about the process, come up with a new one.

Find one question about your role in the decision. If you don't have a question about your role, come up with a new one.

Reflecting
What value do you see in asking questions about the reasons for a decision?
What value do you see in asking questions about the process for making a decision?
What could happen if you ask questions about the reason and the process but do not ask about your role?
What did you learn?
How can you use it?

The Support, Monitor, and Advocate Model

Time: 7 minutes with individuals; 15 minutes with groups

Handouts: Support, Monitor, Advocate: Three Roles Parents Can Play in Their Children's Education; Support, Monitor, and Advocate Action Plan

Process:

1. Give a brief overview of the exercise. Let participants know that you will be introducing some ideas about how to partner with the school and asking them to think about those ideas.

2. Introduce and discuss one role at a time. Define terms, and ask parents to name how they are playing each role.

Role	Facilitation Tips
Define Support In this role, parents help, encourage, and provide for their children. They also support the work of teachers and the school on behalf of their children Ask parents to think about the different activities they are doing to support their children's education.	This activity can be facilitated as a full activity for parents to explore the roles or as an introduction in which definitions and examples of the roles are provided to develop awareness. Use the Support, Monitor, and Advocate Action Plan as a handout for this activity. Parents can also complete the action plan on their own. Two examples of how parents are playing each role will be sufficient.

Define Monitor
   In this role, parents keep track of their children's progress and pay attention to their children's needs.
   They monitor their children's entire school experience, how they are doing academically and socially, and how the school is meeting their needs.
   Ask parents to think about the different activities they are doing to monitor their children's education.
	You can give examples of how each role can be played after parents have thought about them.

Define Advocate
   As advocates, parents make specific requests on behalf of their children. They can also address issues individually or as part of an organized group at the classroom, school, and district levels.
   Ask parents to think about examples of how they have advocated for their children.
	It is likely that parents will be playing this role the least or not playing it actively. If parents get stuck with this role, you can ask them to think about how they have advocated at the school or in other settings.

Ask parents to name one additional activity they would like to do to play each of the roles.	They can use the template on page 207.

3. Ask parents to share out if they are working in small groups.

4. Ask parents to reflect on two or more of the following questions. Introduce one question at a time. Parents can reflect individually and share in small groups or as part of a large group. The reflection allows parents to review the process and think about further application. Try your best not to skip this step.

   » What could happen if you support your child but don't monitor his or her progress?

> » What could happen if you support and monitor but don't advocate?
> » What did you learn?
> » How can you use it?

General Facilitation Tips

When you facilitate the activity on the three roles, parents can work in small groups or in teams of two and then share with each other or in the large group. Allow parents to share examples of how they are playing the roles before naming additional activities to support, monitor, and advocate.

Sample Facilitation Timeframes

Here are approximate times for facilitating the activity with individuals and groups of parents. You can facilitate the process with individual parents in as little as 7 minutes. Groups can complete the activity in about 15 minutes.

The Support, Monitor, and Advocate Model: Sample Timeframe

Process	7 Minutes	15 Minutes
Defining the roles (support, monitor, advocate) and identify how parents are playing the roles	4	6
Sharing out	—	2
Naming one additional activity parents will do to support, monitor, and advocate	2	3
Sharing out	—	2
Reflecting	1	2

Support, Monitor, and Advocate: Three Roles Parents Can Play in Their Children's Education

Role 1: SUPPORT

Parents

- Meet their children's basic health, nutritional, and emotional needs.
- Communicate that they consider education a priority and create space and time for children to do schoolwork at home.
- Do their best to ensure students arrive safely to school and return safely home.
- Support the work of teachers and the school on behalf of their children.

Role 2: MONITOR

Parents

- Keep track of their children's progress.
- Pay attention to their children's needs.
- Monitor their children's entire school experience.
- Monitor how they are doing academically and socially.
- Monitor how the school is meeting their needs.

Role 3: ADVOCATE

Parents

- Speak up and make specific requests on behalf of their children.
- Act as advocates for meeting the needs of all children.
- Address issues individually or as part of an organized group at the classroom, school, and district levels.

Developing an Action Plan

To *support* my child, I'm currently doing the following:

These are two activities I'm currently doing to *monitor* my child:

This is one example of how I currently *advocate* or have advocated for my child:

Support, Monitor, and Advocate Action Plan

This is one additional activity I would like to do to support, monitor, and advocate on behalf of my child:

To support, I will	To monitor, I will	To advocate, I will

I learned that:

Tips for Designing a Question Focus

> *Question Focus: A statement, phrase, problem, or visual aid that serves as the focus for asking questions.*

The Question Focus is more effective when presented as a brief statement, picture, or simple problem to solve. It can be anything, but it should *not* be a question. If the Question Focus is a question, parents will try to find answers to the question rather than think broadly and creatively.

Process for Designing a Question Focus

Keep the end goal of the session in mind when choosing a Question Focus. Think about how the questions will be used. For example, do you need a Question Focus for group and individual educational purposes or for problem solving?

The process for designing the Question Focus includes some easy steps:

1. Name the topic, problem, or situation.
2. Name the type of Question Focus. Is this for asking questions in general or for asking questions about decisions?
3. Think about your purpose. Why do you want participants to ask questions?
4. Name how the questions produced will be used.
5. Generate three ideas related to the topic.
6. Choose the idea you think will best stimulate questioning.
7. Test them out by asking your own questions.
8. Evaluate the chosen idea. Make changes based on the criteria that are not met.

Designing an effective Question Focus is key to engaging parents in asking questions. The Question Focus can be any of the following:

Real-Life Situations
- The child might need to go to summer school.
- The child is struggling in school.
- New school policies on grading will be explored.

Imaginary Situations
- Imagine that the child will be held back in the same grade.
- Imagine that the child is not making expected progress.
- Imagine there are changes on how progress will be assessed.

Educational Topics or Situations
- Academic standards.
- Assessment and grading.
- Improving the school environment.

Two different types of Question Focus are used with parents: one intended to produce questions in general, and one intended to produce questions about decisions. For the former, the goal is for parents to ask questions about any topic or situation, such as homework, school assignments, the classroom environment, or some of the issues in the previous examples.

For the latter type, the goal is for parents to ask questions about decisions. This type must include a decision. Examples include the following:

- Your child has been referred for an IEP.
- Your child will be held back in the same grade for one more year.
- The decision to refer your child for an IEP.
- The decision to hold back your child for one more year.

Designing Tips

Make the Question Focus relevant. The QFocus becomes more relevant and engaging when it is personalized and parents see a direct impact on their child or themselves. For instance, "Child has been referred for an IEP" or "Child is struggling in school" can become more relevant if they are written to include the phrase *your child*: "Your child has been referred for an IEP" or "Your child is struggling in school."

Sharpen the Question Focus. Make it as specific as possible. An example such as "Changes at the school" is too broad. To make it more focused, name specific types of changes (e.g., curriculum, staff, administrative) and when the changes will take place. For example, "There will be changes in what your child will learn this year in math class" or "The school day will be structured differently this year."

Question Focus Design Template

Name the topic, problem, or situation.	
Identify the Question Focus type.	This Question Focus is related to ___ an actual issue. ___ a possible issue/challenge. ___ a general topic of interest to participants. ___ a decision. ___ other: _____
Name the purpose of the Question Focus.	The Question Focus will facilitate ___ problem solving. ___ specific actions. ___ a greater understanding of an educational issue. ___ other: _____
Identify how the questions will be used.	The questions will ___ be answered immediately. ___ help set a learning agenda. ___ serve as a basis for problem solving. ___ identify information needed. ___ be used to demonstrate the process of asking better questions. ___ other: _____
List three brief statements or ideas you can use as a Question Focus.	Statements or ideas to engage participant(s) in asking questions about the topic or problem: 1. 2. 3.

Choose the idea you think will be most effective for stimulating questions.	Idea chosen: # _____ What is your reason for choosing this idea?
Test it out.	Ask questions about the idea chosen.
Assess the effectiveness of the Question Focus.	This Question Focus idea Yes　　　No 　___　　　___ is relevant to the participant(s). 　___　　　___ is brief and engaging. 　___　　　___ elicits questions easily. 　___　　　___ has a clear focus. 　___　　　___ is not a question. If you answered *no*, what changes will you make?
Identify the final version of the Question Focus.	

Planning to Integrate the Right Question Strategy into School Activities

Name how the questions will be used.	The questions will be used to:
Choose or design a Question Focus.	(Reference the Question Focus Design Template for instructions.)
Choose QFT steps to be facilitated.	QFT Steps: ___ Discuss the rules for producing questions. ___ Identify closed- and open-ended questions. ___ Name advantages and disadvantages of closed- and open-ended questions. ___ Change questions from one type to the other. ___ Prioritize questions. ___ Share next steps. ___ Reflect.
Name prioritization instructions.	Name your instructions for choosing the priority questions. Keep the purpose of the activity in mind when doing so. For example, "Choose three questions you would like to address first" or "Choose the three questions that are most important for you."
Name how the priority questions will be shared.	___ Groups will report to one another. ___ Priority questions will be shared in the large group. ___ Other:_____
Name what you will tell participants will be done with the questions.	This is what we will do with the questions . . .
Name reflection questions.	For example, "What did you learn? What value does it have? How can you use it?"

Framework for Accountable Decision Making

Define the term *decision*.	
Examples of everyday decisions you will use.	
Question Focus *(The QFocus must include a decision.)*	
Choose QFT steps you will use.	__ Discuss the rules for producing questions. __ Categorize questions. __ Prioritize. *(optional)*
Instructions for prioritizing questions about reason, process, and role.	
Next steps with the questions.	

Support, Monitor, and Advocate

Introduce the three roles.	__ Before the QFT __ After the QFT __ Before the Framework for Accountable Decision Making __ As a closing activity __ Other: _____
How will parents work?	__ Individually __ In small groups __ Other: _____

Steps parents will follow.	__ Name how they are supporting, monitoring, and advocating.
	__ Name an additional activity they will do to support, monitor, and advocate.
	__ Share with one another how they are playing the roles.
	   __ Teams of two
	   __ Small groups
	   __ Large group
	   __ Will not share
	__ Reflect.

The Question Formulation Technique and Thinking Abilities

The Question Formulation Technique (QFT) not only invests in people's ability to ask their own questions—instead of giving them questions to ask—but also manages to develop three distinct thinking abilities in just one process.

- *Divergent thinking* is the ability to think broadly and creatively. Divergent thinking occurs during the QFT's first step when parents produce their own questions related to the Question Focus. This gives them space and license to ask any question that comes to mind, thus encouraging divergent thinking. The process is very productive in a group setting where parents hear questions they would not have thought of themselves and are stimulated to think in new ways.

- *Convergent thinking* is the ability to narrow down and synthesize. Convergent thinking in the QFT begins when parents examine their close- and open-ended questions and practice changing them from one type to the other. As they do this, they often note how asking a question in a certain way can yield different information and draws their attention to the deliberate construction of a question for specific purposes. Convergent thinking continues to develop as they prioritize their questions. Trying to assess which three should be their priority questions, pushes them to examine each question more closely and to think more deeply about the relative value of each one. They analyze their questions, obtain new insights and often discover that some of the first questions that came to mind cannot be answered until they get answers to questions that appear later on their list. This leads to a deeper understanding of the power of first producing and then late analyzing their questions. Then, as they plan their next steps their convergent thinking ability grows stronger and they strategize about specific uses of their questions.

- *Metacognition* is the ability to think about one's own thinking. Parents develop their metacognitive thinking ability at various points in the whole process. Right at the start of the process they think about and discuss what might be difficult about following the four rules for producing questions. This pushes them to consider how they normally ask questions, or even how rarely they deliberately work on asking their own questions. They then consider and discuss the advantages and disadvantages of close- and open-ended questions that lead to new insights about the nature of questions. When they get to the end of the process and are encouraged to reflect on what they have learned and even how they learned it, they are now more conscious of their own thinking processes, the value of working with questions and how rigorous thinking through questions can lead to their feeling more capable and confident. The metacognitive work at the very end is crucial for reinforcing the intellectual growth that has taken place through the QFT process.

References

Alegría, M., Polo, A., Gao, S., Santana, L., Rothstein, D., Jimenez, A., Hunter, M. L., Mendieta, F., Oddo, V., & Normand, S. L. (2008). Evaluation of a patient activation and empowerment intervention in mental health care. *Med Care, 46*(3), 247–256.

Alexander, M. (2010). *The New Jim Crow: Mass incarceration in the age of color blindness.* New York: New Press.

Andrews, T. J., Wisniewski, J. J., & Mulick, J. A. (1997). Variables influencing teachers' decisions to refer children for school psychological assessment services. *Psychology in the Schools, 34*(3), 239–244.

Arnstein, S. (1969). A ladder of citizen participation. *AIP Journal,* 216–224.

Asera, R. (2001, May). Calculus and community: A history of the emerging scholars program. *The College Board,* 1–40.

Auerbach, S. (2009). Walking the walk: Portraits in leadership for family engagement in urban schools. *School Community Journal, 19*(1), 9–32.

Bandura, A. (2001). Social cognitive theory: An agentic perspective. *Annual Review of Psychology, 52*(1), 1–26.

Berger, W. (2014). *A more beautiful question: The power of inquiry to spark breakthrough ideas.* New York: Bloomsbury.

Black, B. (1998). *Massachusetts parent training and empowerment project evaluation report: Years one and two.* (Almeida, C.A., Ed). (pp. 1–30).

Blanchett, W. (2006). Disproportionate representation of African American students in special education: Acknowledging the role of White privilege and racism. *Educational Researcher, 35*(6), 24–28.

Breiseth, L., Robertson, K., & Lafond, S. (2011). A guide for engaging ELL families: Twenty strategies for school leaders. *Colorin Colorado.*

C3 Teachers. (n.d.). C3 teachers: Inquiry design model. Retrieved from www.c3teachers.org/inquiry-design-model/

Deen, D., Lu, W. H., Rothstein, D., Santana, L., & Gold, M. R. (2011). Asking questions: The effect of a brief intervention in community health centers on patient activation. *Patient Education and Counseling, 84*(2), 257–260.

Dewey, J. (1916). *Democracy and education: An introduction to the philosophy of education.* New York: Macmillan.

Drucker, P. F. (1954). *The practice of management: A study of the most important function in American society.* New York: HarperBusiness.

Duncan, G. J., & Murnane, R. J. (2014). *Restoring opportunity: The crisis of inequality and the challenge for American education.* Cambridge, MA: Harvard Education Press.

Durlak, J. A., Weissberg, K. B., Dymnicki, A. B., Taylor, R. D., & Schellinger, R. P. (2011). The impact of enhancing students' social and emotional learning: A meta-analysis of school-based universal interventions. *Child Development, 82*(1), 405–432.

Editorial Projects in Education Research Center. (2011). Issues A–Z: Achievement gap. *Education Week.* Retrieved from www.edweek.org/ew/issues/achievement-gap/

Edmonds, R. (1979). Effective schools for the urban poor. *Educational Leadership, 37*(1), 15–24.

Elias, M. (2013). The school-to-prison pipeline [Web log post]. Retrieved from www.tolerance.org/magazine/number-43-spring-2013/school-to-prison

Epstein, J. (2001). *School, family, and community partnerships: Preparing educators and improving schools.* Boulder, CO: Westview.

Ferlazzo, L., & Hammond, L. A. (2009). *Building parent engagement in schools.* Columbus, OH: Linworth Books/Libraries Unlimited.

Garrett, R. T. (1997, August 24). Poor parents can learn to work the system, too. *Courier-Journal* [Louisville].

Harvard Graduate School of Education. (n.d.). Data Wise. Retrieved from http://isites.harvard.edu/icb/icb.do?keyword=datawise

Harvard Medical School. (2015). *Academy annual symposium on the science of learning. Dealing with failure: Getting our learners to ask the right questions* [Pamphlet]. Cambridge, MA: Harvard Medical School.

Haskins, R., & Adams, D. (Eds.). (1983). *Parent education and public policy.* Norwood, NJ: Ablex.

Henderson, A., & Mapp, K. (2002). A new wave of evidence: The impact of school, family, and community connections on student achievement. *SEDL, Annual Synthesis,* 1–234.

Henderson, A. T., Mapp, K. L., Johnson, V. R., & Davies, D. (2007). *Beyond the bake sale: The essential guide to family-school partnerships.* New York: New Press.

High Expectations Parental Service & Partnership for Children & Youth (2013a). *Why family engagement matters.* California: Author.

High Expectations Parental Service & Partnership for Children & Youth. (2013b). *Student supports: Getting the most out of your LCFF investment.* California: Author.

Hong, S., & Anyon, J. (2011). *A cord of three strands: A new approach to parent engagement in schools.* Cambridge, MA: Harvard Education Press.

Hoover-Dempsey, K. V., & Sandler, H. M. (1997). Why do parents become involved in their children's education? *Review of Educational Research, 67*(1), 3–42.

Jackson, E., & Turner, C. (2015). *Unique challenges in urban schools: The involvement of African American parents.* Lanham, MD: Rowman & Littlefield.

Kammen, K., Krizic, M., Lewis, M., Peterson, R., Prahl, L., Shadowens, J., & Thao, P. (2014). Family engagement for educational achievement acceleration (Masters capstone). *University of Minnesota Digital Conservancy.*

Karchmer, A. (2010). *Right question institute training for the Bedouin women's empowerment project.* Presentation in Beersheva, Israel.

Katz, B. (2015). The individualized education program process in special education. Retrieved from www.specialeducationguide.com/pre-k-12/individualized-education-programs-iep/the-iep-process-explained/

Kellogg Foundation. (2013). *Family engagement: A shared responsibility among families, schools, and communities.* Retrieved from https://wrm.wkkf.org/uwebrequestmanager/ui/wkkffamilyengagement_request_for_submission_final.pdf

Kupper, L. (Ed.). (2000). Archived: Guide to the individualized education program. Retrieved from http://www2.ed.gov/parents/needs/speced/iepguide/index.html#introduction

Lareau, A. (2003). *Unequal childhoods: Class, race, and family life.* Berkeley: University of California Press.

Lawrence-Lightfoot, S. (2003). *The essential conversation: What parents and teachers can learn from each other.* New York: Random House.

Lu, W. H., Deen, D., Rothstein, D., Santana, L., & Gold, M. R. (2011). Activating community health center patients in developing question-formulation skills: A qualitative study. *Health Education & Behavior, 38*(6), 637–645.

Mapp, K. (2003). Having their say: Parents describe why and how they are engaged in their children's learning. *School Community Journal,* 35–64.

Mapp, K. (2011, September 7). Feature: A conversation with Dr. Karen Mapp, consultant on family engagement [Interview by A. Hinton].

Mapp, K. L., & Kuttner, P. J. (2013). *Partners in education: A dual capacity-building framework for family-school partnerships.* SEDL.

McKinsey & Company. (2009). *The economic impact of the achievement gap in America's schools.* New York: Author.

Minow, M. (2001). Justine Wise Polier Memorial Lecture: In the meantime: The gap between promises and realities for kids. Harvard Law School, Cambridge, MA.

Molnar, M. (2013). Boston leader connects parents to learning. *Education Week: Leaders to Learn From.*

Nelson, P. (2003). Questions: A powerful tool for self-advocacy. *The Change Agent, 16,* 20.

NGSS Lead States. (2013). *Next Generation Science Standards: For states, by states.* Washington, DC: National Academies Press.

No Child Left Behind Act of 2001, Pub. L. No. 107-110, 115 Stat. 1425 (2001).

Olinger, R., & Nelson, K. (2015). *The right question: Effective patient strategy (RQ-EPS): Increasing patient engagement in health care.* Kaiser Permanente Webinar.

Prichard Committee for Academic Excellence. (2012). Prichard committee for academic excellence. Retrieved from www.prichardcommittee.org

Rothstein, D. (2012, January 13). Setting off and sustaining sparks of curiosity and creativity [Blog post]. Retrieved from The Blog of Harvard Education Publishing website: http://hepg.org/blog/setting-off-and-sustaining-sparks-of-curiosity-and

Rothstein, D., & Santana, L. (2011). *Make just one change: Teach students to ask their own questions.* Cambridge, MA: Harvard Education Press.

Rothstein, D., Santana, L., & Minigan, A. P. (2015). Making questions flow. *Educational Leadership, 73*(1), 70–75.

Ruscoe, G., & Gaus, D. (1997). *Building parents' skills to support, monitor and advocate for their children's education: Evaluation data from right question workshops in Louisville, Kentucky* (pp. 1–8).

Schott Foundation for Public Education. (n.d.). Opportunity gap: Talking Points. Retrieved from http://schottfoundation.org/issues/opportunity-gap/talking-points

Sexton, R. F. (2004). *Mobilizing citizens for better schools.* New York: Teachers College Press.

Smith, B. H., & Low, S. (2013). The role of social-emotional learning in bullying prevention efforts. *Theory into Practice, 52*(4), 280–287.

TC Media Center. (2005). The academic achievement gap: Facts and figures. Retrieved from www.tc.columbia.edu/news.htm?articleID=5183

Teller, E. (1954, September 6). Dr. Edward Teller's magnificent obsession. *Life,* 61–74.

Treisman, U. (1992). Studying students studying calculus: A look at the lives of minority mathematics students in college. *College Mathematics Journal, 23*(5), 362–372.

U.S. Department of Education. (2009). *Family and community engagement.* Washington, DC: Author.

U.S. Department of Education Office for Civil Rights. (2014). *Civil Rights data collection: Data snapshot (school discipline)* (Issue Brief No. 1). Retrieved from www2.ed.gov/about/offices/list/ocr/docs/crdc-discipline-snapshot.pdf

Walker, E. (2006). Urban high school students' academic communities and their effects on mathematics success. *American Educational Research Journal, 43*(1), 43–71.

Warren, M. R. (2001). *Dry bones rattling: Community building to revitalize American democracy.* Princeton, NJ: Princeton University Press.

Weiss, H. B., Kreider, H. M., Lopez, M. E., & Chatman-Nelson, C. M. (2005). *Preparing educators to involve families: From theory to practice.* Los Angeles: SAGE.

Zernike, K. (2002, August 4). Tests are not just for kids. *The New York Times.* Retrieved from www.nytimes.com/2002/08/04/education/tests-are-not-just-for-kids.html

Index

The letter *f* following a page number denotes a figure.

About the Authors

We have greatly benefited from the diversity of experiences and backgrounds that we bring to our team.

 **Luz Santana** is the codirector of the Right Question Institute and the coauthor of *Make Just One Change: Teach Students to Ask Their Own Questions* (2011). In the late 1980s, as a parent of children in the Lawrence, MA, public school system, she began to work with other parents as part of a drop-out prevention program. At the time, she was also traveling a path that led from her own personal experiences coming from Puerto Rico and then navigating the welfare and other public systems and continuing on to getting an associate's degree to a bachelor's and a master's degree from Springfield College School of Human Services. One of the founders of the Right Question Institute, she is now a nationally recognized educational innovator, facilitator, and keynote speaker in English and Spanish who has designed a

wide range of participatory learning curricula in many fields, including parent involvement, adult education, social services, health care, immigrant advocacy, neighborhood organizing, and voter engagement. Her work has been featured in the *Boston Globe*, international press in Spanish, and on National Public Radio.

Dan Rothstein is the codirector of the Right Question Institute and coauthor of *Make Just One Change: Teach Students to Ask Their Own Questions* (2011). He is a former National Academy of Education Spencer Fellow and earned a doctorate from the Harvard Graduate School of Education before becoming the director of neighborhood planning for the City of Lawrence, MA. He was one of the founders of the Right Question Institute (formerly known as the "Right Question Project") and has collaborated with Luz Santana and other staff at the Right Question Institute to create curricula, teaching materials, articles, and books that are widely used to support adoption of the Right Question Strategy. His work has been featured on NPR and other media outlets, and he is a frequent presenter and keynote speaker at national conferences and symposia.

Agnes S. Bain is a lifelong resident of Lawrence, MA, and began work with Santana and Rothstein when she was a parent of children in the Lawrence public schools system. She is one of the founders (and a past president and current board member) of the Right Question Institute. She has helped develop the institute's original concept of micro-democracy and has contributed to innovative teaching materials and resources for promoting greater citizen participation on all levels of a democratic society. She has a PhD from Boston University and is a professor of government at Suffolk University where she has taught courses on community advocacy and topics in democracy. Agnes's kitchen table has a special place in Right Question Institute history as the location where some of its best ideas and curricula were first developed.

Related ASCD Resources

At the time of publication, the following ASCD resources were available (ASCD stock numbers in parentheses). For up-to-date information about ASCD resources, go to **www.ascd.org**. This book relates to the **supported** tenet of ASCD's Whole Child Initiative; to learn more about this initiative, go to **www.ascd.org/wholechild**. Search the complete archives of *Educational Leadership* at **www.ascd.org/el**.

ASCD Edge®
Exchange ideas and connect with other educators on the social networking site ASCD Edge at http://ascdedge.ascd.org/

Print Products
Building Teachers' Capacity for Success: A Collaborative Approach for Coaches and School Leaders by Pete Hall & Alisa Simeral (#109002)

Everyday Engagement: Making Students and Parents Your Partners in Learning by Katy Ridnouer (#109009)

Insights into Action: Successful School Leaders Share What Works by William Sterrett (#112009)

Mobilizing the Community to Help Students Succeed by Hugh B. Price (#107055)

The New Principal's Fieldbook: Strategies for Success by Pam Robbins and Harvey Alvy (#103019)

The Principal Influence: A Framework for Developing Leadership Capacity in Principals by Pete Hall, Deborah Childs-Bowen, Ann Cunningham-Morris, Phyllis Pajardo, & Alisa A. Simeral (#116026)

Reaching Out to Latino Families of English Language Learners by David Campos, Rocio Delgado, and Mary Esther Soto Huerta (#110005)

Turning High-Poverty Schools into High-Performing Schools by William H. Parrett and Kathleen M. Budge (#109003)

For more information: send e-mail to member@ascd.org; call 1-800-933-2723 or 703-578-9600, press 2; send a fax to 703-575-5400; or write to Information Services, ASCD, 1703 N. Beauregard St., Alexandria, VA 22311-1714 USA.